History–Social Science Framework

for California Public Schools
Kindergarten Through Grade Twelve

Developed by the
**History–Social Science Curriculum
Framework and Criteria Committee**

Adopted by the
California State Board of Education
*in July, 1987, during
the year of the Bicentennial
of the United States Constitution*

Publishing Information

When the *History–Social Science Framework for California Public
Schools* was adopted by the California State Board of Education on July
10, 1987, the members of the Board were: Perry Dyke, President; Francis
Laufenberg, Vice-President; Joseph D. Carrabino; Agnes Chan; Gloria
Hom; Susan Owens, Student Member; Angie Papadakis; Kenneth L.
Peters; Jim C. Robinson; David T. Romero; and Armen Sarafian.

The framework was developed by the History–Social Science Curriculum
Framework and Criteria Committee. (See pages ix–xii for the membership
of the full committee and the names of the principal writers and others
who made significant contributions to the document.) The framework was
edited by Mirko Strazicich, working in cooperation with Diane Brooks.
The document was prepared for photo-offset production by the staff of the
Bureau of Publications, California Department of Education, with artwork
and layout design by Paul Lee. Typesetting was done by Anna Boyd and
Leatrice Shimabukuro.

The framework was published by the California Department of Education,
721 Capitol Mall, Sacramento, California (mailing address: P.O. Box
944272, Sacramento, CA 94244-2720). It was printed by the Office of
State Printing and distributed under the provisions of the Library
Distribution Act and *Government Code* Section 11096.

ISBN 0-8011-0712-1

Ordering Information

Copies of this publication are available for $7.75 each, plus sales tax for
California residents, from the Bureau of Publications, Sales Unit,
California Department of Education, P.O. Box 271, Sacramento, CA
95812-0271; FAX (916) 323-0823. See page 122 for complete information on payment, including credit card purchases.

A list of other publications available from the Department appears on
pages 121 and 122. A complete list may be obtained by writing to the
address given above or by calling the Sales Unit at (916) 445-1260.

ontents

$\mathscr{S}$tate Board's Message

The State Board of Education is pleased to present the *History–Social Science Framework for California Public Schools, Kindergarten Through Grade Twelve* to educators. This framework represents a consensus on history–social science education among those who prepared the document: teachers, curriculum specialists, administrators, and faculty from institutions of higher education.

We believe that this framework will be useful to those responsible for curriculum planning at the local level for schools and districts. The State Board of Education is required by the Constitution of the State of California to adopt textbooks for students in kindergarten through grade eight, and our intent is that this framework influence the development of instructional materials at all levels, kindergarten through grade twelve.

Our appreciation is extended to each member of the History–Social Science Curriculum Framework and Criteria Committee. The direction provided by this committee has produced a framework that will help students in this state understand the significance of the past and its meaning for their lives today. We express our thanks to the Curriculum Development and Supplemental Materials Commission, especially the History–Social Science Subject Matter Subcommittee and the State Department of Education staff for their roles in developing this framework. We also take this opportunity to express our appreciation to the writers of this framework who carefully and thoughtfully recorded the recommendations and addressed issues of concern to all of us.

We must communicate to students, teachers, parents, and the community that the study of history is not only important but rewarding, too. The State Board of Education wants all students to benefit from a history–social science program that will encourage good citizenship and a commitment to democratic values.

PERRY DYKE, President
FRANCIS LAUFENBERG, Vice-President
JOSEPH D. CARRABINO
AGNES CHAN
GLORIA HOM
SUSAN OWENS

ANGIE PAPADAKIS
KENNETH L. PETERS
JIM C. ROBINSON
DAVID T. ROMERO
ARMEN SARAFIAN

Foreword

I am very proud of this framework for the history–social science curriculum. It is a direct and powerful answer to widespread public demand for a revival of the teaching of history and geography. This framework places history at the center of the social sciences and humanities, where it belongs; history is the glue that makes the past meaningful, the lens through which children and adults can come to understand the world that they live in and understand how it was shaped.

This new framework aims to establish a sequential curriculum, so that all of our children will develop understanding and knowledge about their own nation and about the other major civilizations in the world. The framework contains a number of commendable features: it integrates history and geography with the humanities and the social sciences; it enriches the content of the early grades; it teaches democratic values and holds them up as a measure against which we may judge ourselves as well as others; it treats ethical ideas seriously and examines their consequences; it acknowledges the importance of both religious and secular ideas as influences on history; it accords three years to the study of world history, more than does any other state curriculum in the nation; it recognizes the multicultural character of American society, now and in the past; it teaches the responsibilities and rights of citizens and encourages student participation in civic and political agencies; and it incorporates the teaching of critical thinking into the content of each course.

Although the framework defines the sequential content for the grades, it encourages teachers to unleash their pedagogical energies in a variety of ways. Where appropriate, teachers will use new technologies, original source documents, debates, simulations, role playing, or whatever means that will bring the students into close encounters with powerful ideas, great events, major issues, significant trends, and the contributions of important men and women.

The framework was distributed not only to teachers, curriculum supervisors, administrators, and college and university faculty throughout California but also to leading educators throughout the nation. The response has been positive. Those who have read the California framework have recognized that it has achieved a remarkable synthesis of American history, interweaving the stories of the many different groups who comprise the American people; that its three-year, chronological treatment of world history far surpasses anything available elsewhere in terms of richness and depth; and that it has successfully incorporated democratic values throughout the curriculum, in every course and every grade.

Unlike many curriculum documents this framework is exciting to read. Many reviewers have written to express their enthusiasm for the vigorous presentation of the course content. Even more encouraging is that many teachers have written to say that they cannot wait to teach it.

This curricular framework will strengthen and enrich what students learn in history and the social sciences not only in California but throughout the nation as well.

Bill Honig

State Superintendent of Public Instruction

Preface

The planning for this document, which was shaped over a two-year period, began with a meeting of the Blue Ribbon Advisory Committee for History Scope and Sequence. This group discussed current research in history–social science; student interest and achievement in the subject; and the current state of curriculum and instruction, textbooks, testing, and teacher training. A series of recommendations for this curricular area resulted from that committee meeting. These recommendations were shared with the History–Social Science Curriculum Framework and Criteria Committee, whose task was to develop a new framework. This committee met monthly for a year.

The Framework Committee determined the basic nature of this framework when it made fundamental decisions about the following issues: the central importance of history; the curricular goals and learning strands; the enriched courses of the early grades; the required number of years for instruction in world and United States history; the thoughtful sequencing of chronological periods of emphasis; the inclusion of different cultural traditions in each year's course; the integration of history and geography and the humanities and social sciences; and the correlation of history–social science with other disciplines. The Framework Committee's draft was submitted to the state's Curriculum Development and Supplemental Materials Commission in January, 1987.

After the Curriculum Commission received the draft document, it was revised on the basis of recommendations from Commission members and the Framework Committee. The draft was then circulated to the field in March, 1987. Approximately 550 copies were sent to selected teachers, administrators, school districts, and offices of county superintendents of schools that represented California's diverse geography and population; to college and university scholars nationwide; and to other educators from many states. The field review produced over 1,700 responses; some were submitted individually and some as group composite reports. Each response was carefully analyzed by the staff of the History–Social Science and Visual and Performing Arts Unit of the California State Department of Education, members of the Curriculum Commission, and the principal writers. As a result of the field reviews, numerous changes and some additions were made to the document.

In June, 1987, the revised draft was unanimously approved by the Curriculum Commission. Further revisions were made in response to requests by the State Board of Education, and in July the framework was adopted unanimously by the State Board of Education.

Appreciation is extended to the many educators and scholars who have contributed to this new History–Social Science Framework during the development and field review processes. Particular thanks are given to the writers of this framework, the Framework Committee, the Curriculum Commission, and staff in the History–Social Science Unit for their dedicated efforts in developing a document that describes an exciting curriculum for students.

District and school administrators and teachers now are responsible for carefully studying the guidelines in this document and assessing: (1) the status of the current curriculum and instruction; and (2) the capacity of existing textbooks and instructional materials to address this new framework. Assessment is followed by planning, curriculum development, and staff training. Since this framework focuses on curriculum integration and correlation and on thoughtful chronological sequencing of course content, the assessment and planning stages should be articulated throughout the grades and across disciplines. Planning is followed by curriculum implementation, which includes selection of textbooks, supporting literature and primary sources, and other instructional materials, and continuing staff development and ongoing evaluation.

Implementation of this framework is central to The Blessings of Liberty: A Constitutional Literacy Initiative. This five-year project is aimed at improving curriculum and instruction, textbooks, other instructional materials, testing, and teacher and administrator training in history–social science. Activities supporting this Initiative have included: a meeting with publishers in July, 1987; a constitutional teachers' institute at UCLA in August, 1987; four regional framework implementation conferences in February, 1988; and a national textbook forum in February, 1988. Additional activities include the development of a model curriculum guide for kindergarten through grade eight, with an accompanying literature list; an update of the *Model Curriculum Standards for Grades Nine Through Twelve;* and the alignment of the statewide testing program for history–social science with the new framework.

Through a well-articulated and planned program, we hope for curriculum and instruction in history–social science that allows for more instructional time and provides opportunity for depth of studies. We hope that, as ambassadors to the next generation, educators are able to use this framework to develop students who have a passion for the subject area and its democratic traditions, who understand the interdependence of the world, and who are effective citizens in a democracy.

JAMES R. SMITH
Deputy Superintendent
Curriculum and Instructional
Leadership Branch

FRANCIE ALEXANDER
Associate Superintendent
Curriculum, Instruction,
and Assessment Division

TOMAS LOPEZ
Director
Office of Humanities
Curriculum Services

DIANE BROOKS
Manager
History–Social Science and
Visual and Performing Arts Unit

Acknowledgments

This framework was developed by the History–Social Science Curriculum Framework and Criteria Committee[1]:

James H. Bell, Teacher, Poway High School, Poway Unified School District

Joyce A. Buchholz, Program Director, World Affairs Council of Northern California

Gary W. Cardinale, Curriculum Coordinator, Corona-Norco Unified School District

Pedro G. Castillo, Associate Professor of History, Oakes College, University of California, Santa Cruz

Todd Clark, Education Director, Constitutional Rights Foundation

Jean T. Claugus, Social Studies Consultant, Sacramento

Jan E. Coleman-Ghilarducci, Teacher and Chairperson of the Social Science Department, Thornton Junior High School, Fremont Unified School District

Charlotte Crabtree, Professor of Education, Graduate School of Education, University of California, Los Angeles

Matthew Downey, Professor of History, Graduate School of Education, University of California, Berkeley

Patricia K. Geyer, Teacher, West Campus, Hiram W. Johnson High School, Sacramento City Unified School District

Michael A. Hulsizer, Curriculum Consultant, Office of the Kern County Superintendent of Schools

Milton A. Kato, Teacher, Thomas Jefferson Upper Elementary School, Madera Unified School District

David L. Levering, Professor of History, California State Polytechnic University, Pomona

Cosetta E. Moore, Social Studies Specialist, Los Angeles Unified School District

Diane Ravitch, Professor of History, Teachers College, Columbia University

Linda K. Reeves, Teacher, Patricia Nixon Elementary School, ABC Unified School District

David I. Reinstein, Principal, Beverly Vista Elementary School, Beverly Hills Unified School District

Alvieri M. Rocca, Teacher, Sequoia Middle School, Redding Elementary School District

---

[1]Titles of the committee members were current when this document was being prepared.

Christopher "Kit" Salter, Professor of Geography, University of California, Los Angeles

Jo-Ann L. Wells-Foster, Coordinator, Elementary Education, Inglewood Unified School District

The principal writers of this document were **Charlotte Crabtree,** Professor of Education, Graduate School of Education, University of California, Los Angeles; and **Diane Ravitch,** Professor of History, Teachers College, Columbia University.

The compiler of the first draft was **Matthew Downey,** Professor of History, Graduate School of Education, University of California, Berkeley.

Appreciation is extended to members of the Blue Ribbon Advisory Committee for History Scope and Sequence, which was established by Superintendent of Public Instruction Bill Honig. The committee members met in January, 1986, to discuss current research and needs in history–social science education and to present suggestions for consideration to the Curriculum Framework and Criteria Committee. The members of the advisory committee were the following:

Zoe Acosta, Director, History–Social Science Curriculum Implementation Center, Office of the Kern County Superintendent of Schools

R. Freeman Butts, Professor Emeritus, Teachers College, Columbia University

Henry Chambers, Professor of Ancient History and Humanities, California State University, Sacramento

Todd Clark, Education Director, Constitutional Rights Foundation, Los Angeles

F. Michael Couch, Teacher, Santa Barbara Senior High School, Santa Barbara High School District

Matthew Downey, Professor of United States History, Graduate School of Education, University of California, Berkeley

Paul Gagnon, Professor of European History, University of Massachusetts

Paula Gillett, Director, Clio Project, Graduate School of Education, University of California, Berkeley

Joyce Harper, Teacher, Manual Arts Senior High School, Los Angeles Unified School District

Milton A. Kato, Teacher, Thomas Jefferson Upper Elementary School, Madera Unified School District

Carol S. Katzman, Director, Educational Services for Kindergarten Through Grade Eight, Beverly Hills Unified School District

David Kennedy, Professor, Department of History, Stanford University

Juan Francisco Lara, Assistant Dean, Graduate School of Education; and Assistant Provost, College of Letters and Science, University of California, Los Angeles

Carol Marquis, Teacher, Monte Vista High School, San Ramon Union High School District

Page Miller, Director, American Historical Association, Washington, D.C.

Diane Ravitch, Professor of History, Teachers College, Columbia University

Christopher "Kit" Salter, Professor of Geography, University of California, Los Angeles

Ted Yanak, Teacher, Miller Junior High School, Cupertino Elementary School District

Participating directly in the preparation of the framework as members of the Curriculum Development and Supplemental Materials Commission were:

Carol S. Katzman, Chairperson of the History–Social Science Subject Matter Subcommittee responsible for developing the framework; and Director of Educational Services for Kindergarten Through Grade Eight, Beverly Hills Unified School District

Ernestine Mazzola, Vice-chairperson of the History–Social Science Subject Matter Subcommittee; and Teacher, Meadow Heights Elementary School, San Mateo City School District

Zoe Acosta, Curriculum Coordinator, Office of the Kern County Superintendent of Schools

Daniel Chernow, Pacific Theatres Corporation, Los Angeles

Charlotte Crabtree, Professor of Education, Graduate School of Education, University of California, Los Angeles

William Habermehl, Assistant Superintendent, Office of the Orange County Superintendent of Schools

Dorothy K. Jackson, Assistant Principal, One Hundred Second Street Elementary School, Los Angeles Unified School District

Bruce C. Newlin, Superintendent, Norwalk-La Mirada Unified School District

The overall processes of framework development were managed by:

Francie Alexander, Associate Superintendent, Curriculum, Instruction, and Assessment Division, California State Department of Education

Diane Brooks, Manager, History–Social Science and Visual and Performing Arts Unit, Office of Humanities Curriculum Services, California State Department of Education

State Department of Education staff members who contributed to the process of developing the framework were:

Ira Clark, Consultant, History–Social Science

Richard Contreras, Consultant, Curriculum Framework and Textbook Development Unit

Jerry Cummings, Consultant, History–Social Science

Tomás Lopez, Director, Office of Humanities Curriculum Services

Harvey Miller, Consultant, History–Social Science

Glen Thomas, Manager, Curriculum Framework and Textbook Development Unit

Support staff included:

Amy Hibbitt, History–Social Science

Jim Lane, History–Social Science

Patti Miller, Office of Humanities Curriculum Services

Linda Vocal, Office of Humanities Curriculum Services

Introduction to the Framework

Introduction to the Framework

By studying history–social science, students will appreciate how ideas, events, and individuals have produced change over time and will recognize the conditions and forces that maintain continuity within human societies.

THE children of California will spend their adult lives in the twenty-first century. As educators we have the responsibility of preparing these children for the challenges of living in a fast-changing society. Their lives, like ours, will be affected by domestic and international politics, economic flux, technological developments, demographic shifts, and the stress of social change. The only prediction that can be made with certainty is that the world of the future will be characterized by continuity and change. The study of continuity and change is, as it happens, the main focus of the history–social science curriculum. The knowledge provided by these disciplines enables students to appreciate how ideas, events, and individuals have intersected to produce change over time as well as to recognize the conditions and forces that maintain continuity within human societies.

As educators in the field of history–social science, we want our students to perceive the complexity of social, economic, and political problems. We want them to have the ability to differentiate between what is important and what is unimportant. We want them to know their rights and responsibilities as American citizens. We want them to understand the meaning of the Constitution as a social contract that defines our democratic government and guarantees our individual rights. We want them to respect the right of others to differ with them. We want them to take an active role as citizens and to know how to work for change in a democratic society. We want them to understand the value, the importance, and the fragility of democratic institutions. We want them to realize that only a small fraction of the world's population (now or in the past) has been fortunate enough to live under a democratic form of government, and we want them to understand the conditions that encourage democracy to prosper. We want them to develop a keen sense

We want our students to understand the value, the importance, and the fragility of democratic institutions . . . to develop a keen sense of ethics and citizenship, and to care deeply about the quality of life in their community, their nation, and their world.

of ethics and citizenship. And we want them to care deeply about the quality of life in their community, their nation, and their world.

The object of the present revision of the history–social science curriculum is to set forth, in an organized way, the knowledge and understanding that our students need to function intelligently now and in the future. Those who prepared this framework believe that knowledge of the history–social science disciplines (history, geography, economics, political science, anthropology, psychology, sociology, and the humanities) is essential in developing individual and social intelligence; preparing students for responsible citizenship; comprehending global interrelationships; and understanding the vital connections among past, present, and future. Without the knowledge that these disciplines convey, our students will be buffeted by changes that are beyond their comprehension. But with a firm grounding in history and the related disciplines, they should have the capacity to make wise choices in their own lives and to understand the swift-moving changes in state, national, and world affairs.

In addition to the knowledge that our students will acquire by studying the human past, they should gain a deep understanding of individual and social ethics. This new framework emphasizes concern for our students' ethical understanding in every grade. We want students to see the connection between ideas and behavior, between the values and ideals that people hold and the ethical consequences of those beliefs. Students should realize that tragedies and triumphs have resulted from choices made by individuals. They should recognize that ideas and actions have real consequences—that history, in other words, is not simply the ebb and flow of impersonal forces but is shaped and changed by the ideas and actions of individuals and governments. We study history not to register high scores in trivia contests but to learn from the sometimes painful, sometimes exhilarating, often humdrum experiences of those who preceded us. We want our students to understand how people in other times and places have grappled with fundamental questions of truth, justice, and personal responsibility and to ponder how we deal with the same issues today. By studying the humanities and examining the ideas of great thinkers, major religions, and principal philosophical traditions, our students will reflect on the various ways that people have struggled throughout time with ethical issues and will consider what the consequences are for us today.

The 13 years of study in which our children are engaged from kindergarten through grade twelve are barely time enough for the educational tasks to be accomplished. Our highly complex society needs well-educated minds and understanding hearts; it needs men and women who understand our political institutions and are prepared to assume the responsibilities of active citizenship. The younger generation needs to understand our history, our institutions, our ideals, our values, our economy, and our relations with other nations in the world. It is commonplace to acknowledge that we live in an interdependent world and function in a global economy. Specifically, we want our students to learn about the cultures, societies, and economic systems that prevail in

We want students to see the connection between ideas and behavior, between the values and ideals that people hold and the ethical consequences of those beliefs.

We want our students to learn about the cultures, societies, and economic systems that prevail in other parts of the world and to recognize the political and cultural barriers that divide people as well as the common human qualities that unite them.

other parts of the world and to recognize the political and cultural barriers that divide people as well as the common human qualities that unite them.

This framework represents an effort to strengthen education in the history–social science curriculum while building on the best practices contained in previous frameworks. The distinguishing characteristics of this framework are as follows:

History, placed in its geographic setting, establishes human activities in time and place.

1 **This framework is centered in the chronological study of history.** History, placed in its geographic setting, establishes human activities in time and place. History and geography are the two great integrative studies of the field. In examining the past and present, students should recognize that events and changes occur in a specific time and place; that historical change has both causes and effects; and that life is bounded by the constraints of place. Throughout this curriculum, the importance of the variables of time and place, when and where, history and geography, is stressed repeatedly.

2 **This framework proposes both an integrated and correlated approach to the teaching of history–social science.** The teacher is expected to integrate the teaching of history with the other humanities and the social science disciplines. The teacher is also expected to work with teachers from other fields, such as the language arts, science, and the visual and performing arts, in order to achieve correlation across subjects. Within the context of this framework, history is broadly interpreted to include not only the political, economic, and social arrangements of a given society but also its beliefs, religions, culture, arts, architecture, law, literature, sciences, and technology.

3 **This framework emphasizes the importance of history as a story well told.** Whenever appropriate, history should be presented as an exciting and dramatic series of events in the past that helped to shape the present. The teacher should endeavor to bring the past to life, to make vivid the struggles and triumphs of men and women who lived in other times and places. The story of the past should be lively and accurate as well as rich with controversies and forceful personalities. While assessing the social, economic, political, and cultural context of events, teachers must never neglect the value of good storytelling as a source of motivation for the study of history.

Studies of history are enriched with the literature of the period and about the period.

4 **This framework emphasizes the importance of enriching the study of history with the use of literature, both literature *of* the period and literature *about* the period.** Teachers of history and teachers of language arts must collaborate to select representative works. Poetry, novels, plays, essays, documents, inaugural addresses, myths, legends, tall tales, biographies, and religious literature help to shed light on the life and times of the people. Such literature helps to reveal the way people saw themselves, their ideas and values, their fears and dreams, and the way they interpreted their own times.

5 **This framework introduces a new curricular approach for the early grades (kindergarten through grade three).** In recognition of the shrinkage of time allotted to history–social science instruction in these grades in the recent past, and the need for deeper content to hold the interest of children, this framework proposes enrichment of the curriculum for these grades. While the neighborhood and the region provide the field for exploratory activities related to geography, economics, and local history, the students will read, hear, and discuss biographies, myths, fairy tales, and historical tales to fire their imagination and to whet their appetite for understanding how the world came to be as it is.

This framework introduces a new curricular approach for the early grades (kindergarten through grade three).

6 **This framework emphasizes the importance of studying major historical events and periods in depth as opposed to superficial skimming of enormous amounts of material.** The integrated and correlated approach proposed here requires time; students should not be made to feel that they are on a forced march across many centuries and continents. The courses in this framework identify specific eras and events that are to be studied in depth so that students will have time to use a variety of nontextbook materials, to think about what they are studying, and to see it in rich detail and broad scope.

This framework emphasizes the study of major historical events and periods in depth.

7 **This framework proposes a sequential curriculum, one in which knowledge and understanding are built up in a carefully planned and systematic fashion from kindergarten through grade twelve.** The sequential development of instruction that proceeds chronologically through the grades will minimize gaps in students' knowledge and avoid unnecessary repetition of material among grades. Teachers in each grade will know what history and social science content and which skills their students have studied in previous years. At each grade level some time will be designated for review of previously studied chronological periods, with attention to differing themes, concepts, or levels of difficulty of understanding.

8 **This framework incorporates a multicultural perspective throughout the history–social science curriculum.** It calls on teachers to recognize that the history of community, state, region, nation, and world must reflect the experiences of men and women and of different racial, religious, and ethnic groups. California has always been a state of many different cultural groups, just as the United States has always been a nation of many different cultural groups. The experiences of all these groups are to be integrated at every grade level in the history–social science curriculum. The framework embodies the understanding that the national identity, the national heritage, and the national creed are pluralistic and that our national history is the complex story of many peoples and one nation, of *e pluribus unum,* and of an unfinished struggle to realize the ideals of the Declaration of Independence and the Constitution.

The history of community, state, region, nation, and world must reflect the experiences of men and women and of different racial, religious, and ethnic groups.

9 This framework increases the place of world history in the curriculum to three years (at grades six, seven, and ten), organized chronologically. While emphasizing the centrality of Western civilizations as the source of American political institutions, laws, and ideology, the world history sequence stresses the concept of global interdependence. Special attention is to be paid to the study of non-Western societies in recognition of the need for understanding the history and cultures of Asian, African, and other non-Western peoples. At each grade level the world history course should integrate the study of history with the other humanities.

10 This framework emphasizes the importance of the application of ethical understanding and civic virtue to public affairs. At each grade level the teacher of history and the social sciences will encourage students to reflect on the individual responsibility and behavior that create a good society, to consider the individual's role in how a society governs itself, and to examine the role of law in society. The curriculum provides numerous opportunities to discuss the ethical implications of how societies are organized and governed, what the state owes to its citizens, and what citizens owe to the state. Major historical controversies and events offer an appropriate forum for discussing the ethics of political decisions and for reflecting on individual and social responsibility for civic welfare in the world today.

11 This framework encourages the development of civic and democratic values as an integral element of good citizenship. From the earliest grades students should learn the kind of behavior that is necessary for the functioning of a democratic society. They should learn sportsmanship, fair play, sharing, and taking turns. They should be given opportunities to lead and to follow. They should learn how to select leaders and how to resolve disputes rationally. They should learn about the value of due process in dealing with infractions, and they should learn to respect the rights of the minority, even if this minority is only a single, dissenting voice. These democratic values should be taught in the classroom, in the curriculum, and in the daily life of the school. Whenever possible, opportunities should be available for participation and for reflection on the responsibilities of citizens in a free society.

Opportunities should be available for participation and for reflection on the responsibilities of citizens in a free society.

12 This framework supports the frequent study and discussion of the fundamental principles embodied in the United States Constitution and the Bill of Rights. In addition to the customary three years of United States history in grades five, eight, and eleven and the course in "Principles of American Democracy" in grade twelve, the history–social science curriculum places a continuing emphasis on democratic values in the relations between citizens and the state. Whether studying United States history or world history, students should be aware of the presence or absence of the rights of the individual, the rights of minorities, the right of the citizen to participate

We must develop in students a continuing concern for democratic values in the relations between citizens and the state.

6

in government, the right to speak or publish freely without governmental coercion, the right to freedom of religion, the right to trial by jury, the right to form trade unions, and other basic democratic rights.

13 **This framework encourages teachers to present controversial issues honestly and accurately within their historical or contemporary context.** History without controversy is not good history, nor is such history as interesting to students as an account that captures the debates of the times. Students should understand that the events in history provoked controversy as do the events reported in today's headlines. Students should try to see historical controversies through the different perspectives of participants. These controversies can best be portrayed by using original documents such as newspapers, court decisions, and speeches that represent different views. Students should also recognize that historians often disagree about the interpretation of historical events and that today's textbooks may be altered by future research. Through the study of controversial issues, both in history and in current affairs, students should learn that people in a democratic society have the right to disagree, that different perspectives have to be taken into account, and that judgments should be based on reasonable evidence and not on bias and emotion.

Through the study of controversial issues, students should learn that judgments should be based on reasonable evidence and not on bias and emotion.

14 **This framework acknowledges the importance of religion in human history.** When studying world history, students must become familiar with the basic ideas of the major religions and the ethical traditions of each time and place. Students are expected to learn about the role of religion in the founding of this country because many of our political institutions have their antecedents in religious beliefs. Students should understand the intense religious passions that have produced fanaticism and war as well as the political arrangements developed (such as separation of church and state) that allow different religious groups to live amicably in a pluralistic society.

Students must become familiar with the basic ideas of the major religious and ethical traditions of each time and place . . . and the role of religion in the founding of this country. . . .

15 **This framework proposes that critical thinking skills be included at every grade level.** Students should learn to detect bias in print and visual media; to recognize illogical thinking; to guard against propaganda; to avoid stereotyping of group members; to reach conclusions based on solid evidence; and to think critically, creatively, and rationally. These skills are to be taught within the context of a curriculum that offers numerous opportunities to explore examples of sound reasoning and examples of the opposite.

16 **This framework supports a variety of content-appropriate teaching methods that engage students actively in the learning process.** Local and oral history projects, writing projects, debates, simulations, role playing, dramatizations, and cooperative learning are encouraged, as is the use of technology to supplement reading and classroom activities and to enrich the teaching of history and social science. Video resources such as video programs and laser discs, computer software, and newly emerging forms of educational technology can provide invaluable resources for the teaching of history, geography, economics, and the other disciplines.

17 **This framework provides opportunities for students' participation in school and community service programs and activities.** Teachers are encouraged to have students use the community to gather information regarding public issues and become familiar with individuals and organizations involved in public affairs. Campus and community beautification activities and volunteer service in community facilities such as hospitals and senior citizen or day care centers can provide students with opportunities to develop a commitment to public service and help link students in a positive way to their schools and communities.

Activities in the school and the community enlarge the classroom learning environment and help students develop a commitment to public service.

Goals and Curriculum Strands

Goals
and Curriculum
Strands

The three major goals are interrelated; none is developed wholly independent of the rest.

THE goals of this *History–Social Science Framework* fall into three broad categories: **Knowledge and Cultural Understanding,** incorporating learnings from history and the other humanities, geography, and the social sciences; **Democratic Understanding and Civic Values,** incorporating an understanding of our national identity, constitutional heritage, civic values, and rights and responsibilities; and **Skills Attainment and Social Participation,** including basic study skills, critical thinking skills, and participation skills that are essential for effective citizenship.

None of these goals is developed wholly independent of the rest. All interact within this curriculum. Study skills and critical thinking skills, for example, are developed through challenging studies in history and the other humanities, geography, and the social sciences. Democratic understandings and civic values are enriched through an understanding of the history of the nation's institutions and ideals. Civic participation requires political knowledge and incurs ethical choice.

The learnings contained in this curriculum can be enriched in countless ways. However, teachers and curriculum developers should be aware that for each of the three major goals, some essential learnings are integral to the development of this history–social science curriculum. These basic learnings serve as curriculum strands, unifying this curriculum across all grades, kindergarten through grade twelve. These basic learnings are first introduced in the primary grades, in simple terms that young children understand, and then regularly reappear in succeeding years, each time deepened, enriched, and extended.

These curriculum strands are a constant in every grade, not options to be added or dropped from one year to the next. In every grade

The curriculum strands are a constant in every grade, and each year these basic learnings are deepened, enriched, and extended.

10

History–Social Science
K—12 Goals and Curriculum Strands

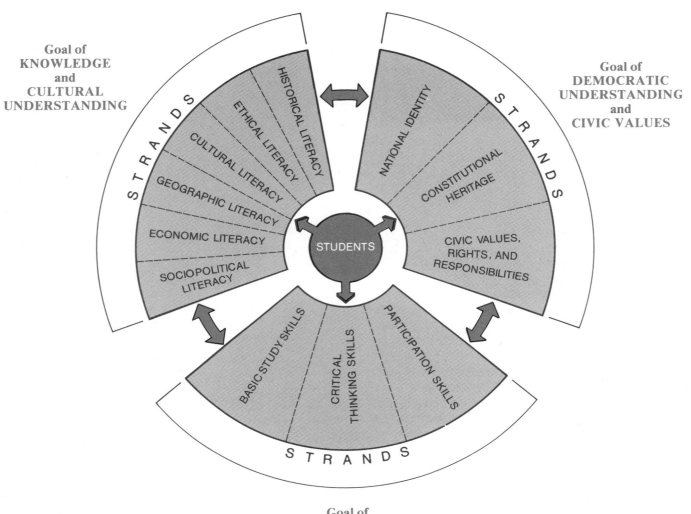

Goal of
**KNOWLEDGE
and
CULTURAL
UNDERSTANDING**

Goal of
**DEMOCRATIC
UNDERSTANDING
and
CIVIC VALUES**

Goal of
**SKILLS ATTAINMENT
and
SOCIAL PARTICIPATION**

11

teachers will be expected to integrate and correlate these strands as part of their teaching of the history–social science curriculum.

In the sections that follow, each of the three goals is presented, together with its basic learnings serving as curriculum strands.

Goal of Knowledge and Cultural Understanding

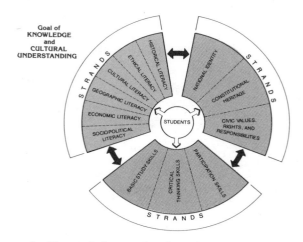

The goal of knowledge and cultural understanding is pursued by developing students' literacy in history and the other humanities (including ethics), geography, economics, sociology, and political science. Certain essential learnings are integral to the development of each of these literacy strands.

Developing literacy in history, the other humanities, and the social sciences is essential to this curriculum.

■ Historical Literacy

To develop historical literacy, students must:

Develop a keen sense of historical empathy. The study of history involves the imaginative reconstruction of the past. Ideally, the student should have a sense of what it was like to be there, to realize that events hung in the balance, that people living then did not know how things ultimately would turn out. Historical empathy is much like entering into the world of a drama, suspending one's knowledge of "the ending" in order to gain a sense of another era and living with the hopes and fears of the people of the time. In every age knowledge of the humanities helps to develop a keen sense of historical empathy by allowing students to see through the eyes of people who were there.

Understand the meaning of time and chronology. History inescapably deals with the dimension of time. Children must learn the meaning of terms such as *decade, generation, century,* and so on. As they grow more mature, students should learn not only when events occurred but also what else was happening at the same time in that society and elsewhere. To define a moment in time (and place) for study is to select a particular set of possibilities and constraints. Chronology defines relationships in time, and students should learn how major events relate to each other in time so that the past is comprehensible rather than a chaotic jumble of disconnected occurrences.

Analyze cause and effect. Integral to the study of history are efforts to understand why things happened and with what consequences; that is, to interpret causes and effects. Historical events usually have multiple causes and multiple effects, some of which are not recognized until long after the event occurs. Students should learn to tell the difference between a cause and a correlation. They also need to understand that the study of causes and effects does not yield cut-and-dried answers because historical interpretation is speculative and subject to change.

Students should learn that historical events usually have multiple causes and effects and that historical interpretation of these causal relationships is open to change.

Understand the reasons for continuity and change. Most of the major events studied in history are examples of change, but it is no less important to recognize why things do not change; in other words, students should understand the sources of continuity. In retrospect certain changes appear to have been inevitable, but students will miss the drama of history if they do not realize that things might have turned out otherwise. What ideas, traditions, and values explain the absence of change? What combination of ideas and events explains the emergence of new patterns?

Recognize history as common memory, with political implications. Throughout recorded time, societies have used their history as a vehicle for maintaining their identity as a people and a nation. The study of history allows people to explain and transmit their ideals and traditions to the younger generation. In tightly controlled societies the historical record may be altered to redefine public consciousness of the past and to regulate the public's loyalties; in democratic societies the historical record is open to debate, revision, conflicting interpretations, and acknowledgment of past mistakes.

Understand the importance of religion, philosophy, and other major belief systems in history. To understand why individuals and groups acted as they did, we must see what values and assumptions they held, what they honored, what they sought, and what they feared. By studying a people's religion and philosophy as well as their folkways and traditions, we gain an understanding of their ethical and moral commitments. By reading the texts that people revere, we gain important insights into their thinking. The study of religious beliefs and other ideological commitments helps explain both cultural continuity and cultural conflict.

By studying a people's religion, philosophy, folkways, and traditions, students gain an understanding of a culture's ethical and moral commitments.

At the core of ethical teaching is respect for each person as a unique individual.

■ Ethical Literacy

To develop ethical literacy, students must:

Recognize the sanctity of life and the dignity of the individual. At the core of ethical teaching is respect for each person as a unique individual. Governmental policies that disregard the value of human life or that condone inhuman practices are unethical. The curriculum offers many opportunities to explore human rights as an ethical issue.

Understand the ways in which different societies have tried to resolve ethical issues. Students should examine the major religious and philosophical traditions in Western and non-Western societies, particularly in their efforts to establish standards of behavior and values for achieving the good life and the good society.

Understand that the ideas people profess affect their behavior. Students should understand the connection between ideas and actions, between ideology and policy, between policy and practice. Whether they are studying the Holocaust or slavery or some other instance of inhumanity, students should recognize the ethical implications of ideology.

Concern for ethics and human rights is universal.

Realize that concern for ethics and human rights is universal and represents the aspirations of men and women in every time and place. Students should be aware of slave revolts in ancient times; of individuals such as Mohandas K. Gandhi who led popular movements for freedom; of Bishop Desmond Tutu, Nobel laureate and outspoken opponent of apartheid; of Christians who risked their lives to save Jews during the Holocaust; of dissidents who risk their lives to reveal the gulags in the U.S.S.R.; and of historic documents such as the United Nations' Universal Declaration of Human Rights.

■ Cultural Literacy

To develop cultural literacy, students must:

Understand the rich, complex nature of a given culture: its history, geography, politics, literature, art, drama, music, dance, law, religion, philosophy, architecture, technology, science, education, sports, social

14

structure, and economy. Cultural literacy includes but is not limited to knowledge of the humanities. True cultural literacy takes many years to develop, whether one is a student of a foreign country or a student of one's own society. Students should not be under the illusion that they truly know another society as a result of studying it for a few weeks or even for a year. At the very least they should learn how difficult it is to master a culture and should be encouraged to recognize that education is a lifelong process.

Recognize the relationships among the various parts of a nation's cultural life. Mature students should come to appreciate the ways that a nation's literature and arts react to and comment on events in its political and social development. They also should study and appreciate the interactions among a nation's governmental system, economic structure, technology, arts, and press. None of the elements of a culture exists in a vacuum, and students will come to understand the connections as they develop a deeper knowledge of the constituent parts.

Learn about the mythology, legends, values, and beliefs of a people. Ideas are important; to understand a society, students must perceive what its members believe about themselves, what stories and tales explain their origins and common bonds, what religious tenets embody their ethical standards of justice and duty, what heroes capture their imagination, what ideals inspire their sense of purpose, and what visual images portray their idea of themselves as a people.

Recognize that literature and art reflect the inner life of a people. Artists and writers tend to have sensitive antennae. In their work artists and writers record the hopes, fears, aspirations, and anxieties of their society. A culture cannot be fully understood without knowledge of the poems, plays, dance, visual art, and other works that express its spirit.

Develop a multicultural perspective that respects the dignity and worth of all people. Students should learn from their earliest school years that our nation is composed of people whose backgrounds are rooted in cultures around the world. They should develop respect for the human dignity of all people and understanding of different cultures and ways of life.

Students should develop respect for the human dignity of all people and understanding of different cultures and ways of life.

■ Geographic Literacy

To develop geographic literacy, students must:

Develop an awareness of place. Geography is fundamentally concerned with the study of place. Historical and contemporary events have occurred in particular places, and generally there are reasons why those

To understand human events, students must first understand the characteristics of the places in which those events occurred.

events unfolded where they did. To understand human events, students must first understand the characteristics of the places in which those events occurred. Physical characteristics of a place include its landforms, water bodies, climate, soils, natural vegetation, and animal life. Human characteristics include the population; the full array of human activities and settlement patterns on the land; the ideological, religious, and philosophical beliefs of its people; and their political and social institutions. In describing a place, students should be able to identify its physical and human characteristics and to explain how these features are interrelated to form the unique character of that place. Through this curriculum students should learn about the earth's continents, the significant countries and cities, the dominant landscape features of the earth, and the physical and cultural contexts in which these places exist.

Develop locational skills and understanding. To study geography, students must be able to use map and globe skills to determine absolute locations in terms of the map grid; determine directions on the earth's surface; measure distances between places; and interpret information available through the map's legend, scale of miles, and symbolic representations.

Students also should be able to judge the significance of the relative location of a place. They should, for example, learn to judge the importance to a settlement of location on a natural harbor or in a fertile river valley, close to a major economic resource, along a major trade route, or in proximity to major markets. As students mature in their geographic thinking, they should learn to analyze how the relative location of a place confers important advantages or disadvantages, consider how these relative advantages or disadvantages can change over time, and determine how such changes have influenced the course of human history in that place.

Understand human and environmental interaction. One of the most dynamic aspects of geographic education is the study of the ways people and environments interact in the human modification of the landscape. From the earliest grades students can examine how people in their neighborhood and locality are "changing the land" by tearing down old structures and building new ones, converting agricultural lands to urban use, or turning desert lands into agricultural oases. Later, students learn that this process of environmental modification in the development of cities, resort areas, and farmlands has been a dominant theme throughout human history. Geographic systems are in constant flux because of both physical and human influences. Natural resources gain value only through human need, and human need changes over time. Students should develop understanding of the major environmental issues confronting modern societies and of the consequences, intentional and unintentional, of human decisions that affect the environment.

Students should develop understanding of major environmental issues and the consequences of human decisions that affect the environment.

Understand human movement. Humans have been on the move since the beginning of history. Students can observe how early humans migrated from place to place in quest of food, water, and security. They can analyze how, later in history, great migrations carried people from one continent to another in the search for places of greater opportunity.

16

They should understand major patterns of domestic and international migration, changing environmental preferences and settlement patterns, and the frictions that develop between population groups from broadly distinct cultural regions. Students should also analyze how much of the landscape of cities and countryside is today marked by transportation networks providing for the continual movement of goods, people, ideas, and information throughout a globally interdependent world. For geographers, this theme is vital because movement promotes the diffusion of ideas, technological innovations, and goods and thereby sets change in motion.

Understand world regions and their historical, cultural, economic, and political characteristics. Geographers cannot deal with all the earth at once. For that reason, the concept of *region* has developed. In this curriculum a local neighborhood may be studied as a region largely composed of Asian or Hispanic immigrants. A Puritan New England colony may be studied as a region largely defined by religious affiliation. Renaissance England or post-World War II America are examples of politically defined regions. The Pacific Basin nations and nations of the North Atlantic Alliance are regions of economic, political, and cultural interaction.

An understanding of the major regions of the Western and non-Western worlds is of major importance if students are to appreciate the growing interdependence and global complexity of their world.

An understanding of the major regions of the Western and non-Western worlds is of major importance if students are to appreciate the growing interdependence and global complexity of their world.

■ Economic Literacy

To develop economic literacy, students must:

Understand the basic economic problems confronting all societies. Basic to all economic decision making is the problem of scarcity. Scarcity requires that all individuals and societies make choices about how to use their productive resources. Students need to understand this basic problem confronting all societies and to examine the ways in which economic systems seek to resolve the three basic economic problems of choice (determining what, how, and for whom to produce) created by scarcity.

Students must understand the basic economic problems confronting all societies.

Understand comparative economic systems. Beginning in the elementary school, students should be introduced to the basic processes through which market economies function and to the growing network of markets and prices that reflect shifting supply and demand conditions in a market economy. In later years students should be able to compare the origins and differentiating characteristics of traditional, command, market, and "mixed" economic systems. Students should understand the mechanisms through which each system functions in regulating the distribution of scarce resources in the production of desired goods and services, and they should analyze their relationships to the social and political systems of the societies in which they function.

Understand the basic economic goals, performance, and problems of our society. Students need to be able to analyze the basic economic goals of their society; that is, freedom of choice, efficiency, equity, full employment, price stability, growth, and security. Students should also recognize the existence of trade-offs among these goals. They need to develop analytical skills to assess economic issues and proposed governmental policies in light of these goals. They also need to know how to explain or describe the performance of the nation's economy. Finally, students need opportunities to examine some of the local, national, and global problems of the nation's mixed economy, including (1) inflationary and deflationary pressures and their effects on workers' real earnings; (2) underemployment and labor; (3) the persistence of poverty in a generally productive economy; (4) the rate of growth and worker production and hence material output; and (5) the successes and failures of governmental programs.

Understand the international economic system. Students need to understand (1) the organization and importance of the international economic system; (2) the distribution of wealth and resources on a global scale; (3) the struggle of the "developing nations" to attain economic independence and a better standard of living for their citizens; (4) the role of the transnational corporation in changing rules of exchange; and (5) the influence of political events on the international economic order.

■ Sociopolitical Literacy

To develop sociopolitical literacy, students must:

Understand the close relationship between social and political systems. To understand the political system of a society, students must also understand the social system. The two systems are interrelated, with the social values of a society reflected in its political institutions. By the time they reach grade ten, students normally are ready to examine social and political relationships; to analyze how social status, social mobility, political power, and prestige are distributed within a society; and to analyze how these factors affect the opportunities that are available to men and women of all walks of life and of all ethnic and racial backgrounds.

Understand the close relationship between society and the law. To understand a society, one must understand the relationship between that society and its laws. In studying the United States, for example, students should come to understand that important public issues and controversies that are not resolved within the social institutions of the society regularly make their way into the political system and the courts for their ultimate resolution. Students should observe that in recent years every major social issue, whether civil rights, equal educational opportunity, abortion, or criminal justice, has reached the courts. They should come to understand that the interpretations of the Constitution reached by the courts are the result of human decisions, which are influenced by changing perceptions of the fit between constitutional principles and social realities. They also should come to understand how judicial decisions, in turn, influence society's goals and values, its institutions, and the attitudes of individual citizens.

Understand comparative political systems. Students should learn about the differences between democratic and nondemocratic political systems, and they should be able to describe the critical characteristics of each system. In analyzing contemporary and historical societies, students should critically examine such questions as how governments gain power over people and land; to what extent power is allocated among citizens and between citizens and government; how governmental power is limited, maintained, and transferred; what protections exist against the abuse of that power; and what provisions exist for the protection of individual and minority rights and freedoms, an independent judiciary and press, and the processes of constitutional choice and the consent of the governed. Finally, students should consider the significance of all the foregoing on the lives of individual citizens.

Students must understand political and social systems, the relationship between a society and its laws, and the differences between democratic and nondemocratic political systems.

Goal of Democratic
Understanding and Civic Values

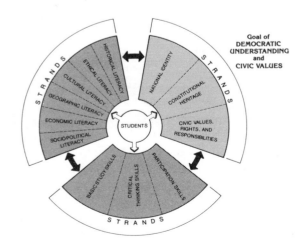

The curricular goal of democratic understanding and civic values is centered on an essential understanding of the nation's identity and constitutional heritage; the civic values that undergird the nation's constitutional order and promote cohesion across all groups in a pluralistic society; and the rights and responsibilities of all citizens.

■ National Identity

To understand this nation's identity, students must:

Recognize that American society is now and always has been pluralistic and multicultural. From the first encounter between indigenous peoples and exploring Europeans, the inhabitants of the North American continent have represented a variety of races, religions, languages, and ethnic and cultural groups. With the passage of time, the United States has grown increasingly diverse in its social and cultural composition. Yet, even as our people have become increasingly diverse, there is broad recognition that we are one people. Whatever our origins, we are all Americans.

Understand the American creed as an ideology extolling equality and freedom. The American creed is derived from the language and values found in the Declaration of Independence, the Constitution, and the Bill of Rights. Its themes are echoed in patriotic songs such as "America the Beautiful" (". . . and crown thy good with brotherhood, from sea to shining sea") and "America" (". . . from every mountainside, let freedom ring"). The creed provides the unifying theme of Martin Luther King, Jr.'s oration, "I Have a Dream": "I have a dream that one day this nation will rise up and live out the true meaning of its creed: *We hold these truths to be self-evident, that all men are created equal. . . .* This will be the day when all of God's children will be able to sing with new meaning, 'My Country, 'Tis of Thee, Sweet Land of Liberty. . . . '" Students should learn the radical implications of such phrases as "all men are created equal" and study the historic struggle to extend to all Americans the constitutional guarantees of equality and freedom.

Recognize the status of minorities and women in different times in American history. Students should be aware of the history of prejudice and discrimination against minorities and women as well as efforts to establish equality and freedom. Students should understand how different minorities were treated historically and should see historical events through a variety of perspectives.

Understand the unique experiences of immigrants from Asia, the Pacific islands, and Latin America. Students should examine the cultural, political, and economic sources of contemporary immigration from these areas to understand the changing demography of California and the United States. Attention should be paid to the contributions of immigrants from Asia, the Pacific islands, and Latin America to life and culture in the United States.

Understand the special role of the United States in world history as a nation of immigrants. The multicultural, multiracial, multiethnic, multireligious character of the United States makes it unusual among the nations of the world. Few, if any, nations can match the United States when compared on a scale of social heterogeneity; few, if any, have opened their doors so wide to immigration and provided such relatively easy access to full citizenship. At the same time students should analyze periodic waves of hostility toward newcomers and recognize that the nation has in different eras restricted immigration on the basis of racial, ethnic, or cultural grounds.

Realize that true patriotism celebrates the moral force of the American idea as a nation that unites as one people the descendants of many cultures, races, religions, and ethnic groups. The American story is unfinished, for it is a story of ideals and aspirations that have not yet been realized. It is a story that is in the making; its main characters are today's students, their parents, and their friends. Unlike other historical events that are wholly in the past, this is a story whose beginning can be traced to the nation's founding and whose outcome rests in the students' hands.

America, as a nation, unites as one people the descendants of many cultures, races, religions, and ethnic groups. The American story is unfinished, and the outcome rests in the students' hands.

■ Constitutional Heritage

To understand the nation's constitutional heritage, students must:

Understand the basic principles of democracy. Students need to understand the central dilemma that confronts all societies and the basic principles that guide the democratic resolution of that dilemma: how to endow civil government with enough power to govern efficiently and yet to limit that power to protect against the tyranny of government and its infringement on the property and liberty of individual citizens. Students need to understand how the Founding Fathers of this nation struggled with these issues and, writing in the context of the American Enlightenment and their religious traditions, framed a Constitution of principles that created a democratic form of government; instituted the rule of law over rulers and the ruled alike; and conferred the basic guarantees of a free society through such fundamental mechanisms as representative government, separation of powers, a system of checks and balances, and limitations on terms of office.

Students must understand the nation's constitutional heritage and the principles of the Constitution that created our democratic form of government.

Students need to understand the principle that democratic government exists for the people and that the people rule through the processes of constitutional choice and consent of the governed.

Students also need to understand the principle that democratic government exists for the people and that the people rule through the processes of constitutional choice and consent of the governed. At the same time students must understand the importance of protecting the rights of minorities against the tyranny of majority rule. They need to develop appreciation for the guarantees provided in the Bill of Rights and for the importance of a democratic system's procedural rules that ensure, for example, due process, a free press, periodic elections, and the peaceable change of government through procedural rules that guarantee that the majority decides. Students also should understand how the Constitution has been amended and improved over time.

Understand the historical origins of basic constitutional concepts such as representative government, separation of powers, and trial by jury. Students need to develop an understanding of the concepts of constitutional government in their historical context. They should examine key documents, including the Magna Carta, the English Bill of Rights, the Mayflower Compact, and the Fundamental Orders of Connecticut, as milestones in the development of democratic government. They need also to study those ideas of the Enlightenment that influenced the authors of the Constitution, especially the ideas of John Locke on natural rights and on the social and government contract; of Charles-Louis Montesquieu on the character of British liberty and the institutional requirements for its attainment; and of Oliver Cromwell's Commonwealth Tradition. Students should understand that the ideas and writings of the leading thinkers of the European Enlightenment were widely quoted in the colonies and that these ideas and writings were discussed by Whigs and Tories alike. This historical context is important for students to understand because it explains the importance of the Constitution as the most enduring monument of the American Enlightenment.

■ Civic Values, Rights, and Responsibilities

To understand civic values, rights, and responsibilities, students must:

Understand what is required of citizens in a democracy. Students must develop understanding of the qualities required of citizens in a democracy. They need to understand, for example, that a democratic society depends on citizens who will take individual responsibility for their own ethical behavior, control inclinations to aggression, and attain a certain level of civility on their own by choosing to live by certain higher rules of ethical conduct. Students need to understand why a democracy needs citizens who value give-and-take on issues, who do not feel it necessary to go to war over every idea, and who seek the middle

Students must understand the qualities and individual responsibilities required of citizens in a democracy for the full realization of this government's highest ideals.

22

ground on which consensus and cooperation can flourish.

Students need also to understand that the democratic process ensures its citizens a field of fair play so one can gracefully accept the loss of a debate or an election on the certain knowledge that there is always the chance to compete again. These are essential insights for students to acquire, for they are the basis for peaceful elections in a democracy, for the orderly transfer of power, and for the readiness of winners and losers alike to join ranks behind the candidate elected in a fair contest. Finally, students need to develop a deep and abiding commitment to democratic values in their individual and social behavior.

Understand individual responsibility for the democratic system. Students need to understand the inherent strengths of the democratic system. But they also need to ponder its fragile nature and the processes through which democracies perish: through erosion of democratic protections; through lack of effective leadership or governance; through indifference of citizens to their rights and responsibilities under the Constitution and the Bill of Rights; through lack of will or courage; through selfishness and alienation; and through usurpation of power by tyrants or antidemocratic extremist groups. Students need to develop appreciation for the informed commitment a democracy requires of its citizens to maintain its basic freedoms. They need to understand that critical thinking and independence of mind are essential characteristics of citizens in a free society and that education develops the critical intelligence necessary for good citizenship. Students need to understand the importance to a democracy of citizens who are willing to participate actively in government, think critically and creatively about issues, confront the unresolved problems of the society, and work through democratic processes toward the fuller realization of its highest ideals in the lives and opportunities of all its citizens.

Students need to understand the inherent strengths of the democratic system and to recognize the processes through which democracies perish.

Goal of Skills Attainment and Social Participation

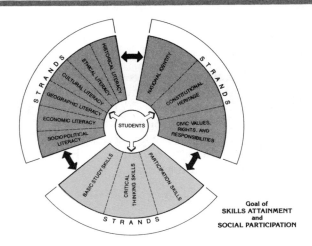

Goal of
SKILLS ATTAINMENT
and
SOCIAL PARTICIPATION

The curricular goal of skills attainment and social participation is pursued by developing students' participation skills, critical thinking skills, and basic study skills.

■ Participation Skills

While the ability to work with others is an asset in any society, it is a requirement for citizenship in a democracy. Democratic government depends on citizens who are actively involved as well as informed. Civic competence requires the skills that make joint effort and effective cooperation possible. It also requires a willingness to work for the common good. As a major conduit by which the democratic heritage is passed to each new generation, the history–social science curriculum must promote the learning of skills that lead to civic competence.

To participate effectively in society, students need to:

Develop personal skills. Among the personal skills that students should develop are sensitivity to the needs, problems, and aspirations of others; the ability to express personal convictions; recognition of personal biases and prejudices; an understanding of people as individuals rather than as stereotypical members of a particular group; and the ability to adjust one's behavior to work effectively with others.

Develop group interaction skills. Among the group interaction skills that students should develop are willingness to listen to the differing views of others; ability to participate in making decisions, setting goals, and planning and taking action in a group setting; leadership skills and the willingness to follow; skills of persuading, compromising, debating, negotiating, and resolving conflicts; and ability to confront controversial issues in ways that work toward reasoned solutions free of aggressions that destroy group relations.

Develop social and political participation skills. Among the social and political participation skills that students should develop are ability to identify issues that require social action; commitment to accept social responsibilities associated with citizenship; willingness to work to influence those in political power to preserve and extend justice, freedom, equity, and human rights; willingness to assume leadership roles in clarifying goals and mobilizing groups for political action; and willingness to accept the consequences of one's own actions.

■ Critical Thinking Skills

The skills involved in critical thinking enable students to question the validity and meaning of what they read, hear, think, and believe. Critical thinking requires a questioning mind and a skeptical withholding of assent about the truth of a statement until it can be critically evaluated. While such skills are developed through everyday living as well as by schooling, the history–social science classroom is an especially appropriate setting for developing such skills. The ability to think critically about public issues, candidates for office, and decisions of government officials is an essential attribute of good citizenship in a democratic society. Students learn critical thinking skills by confronting issues and writing analytical commentaries. In reading documents and other original materials, students have an opportunity to interpret the writer's language and to extract meaning. When original texts such as the Declaration of Independence, the Constitution, or the Seneca Falls Declaration are read to supplement or replace the textbook, critical discussion and thinking are promoted. Writing about the subject matter of history and social science gives students valuable experience in thinking through their ideas and articulating them.

The following critical thinking skills are to be developed in the context of the history–social science curriculum:

Define and clarify problems. Included in these skills are the ability to identify central issues or problems, to determine which information is relevant, to make distinctions between verifiable and unverifiable information or between essential and incidental information, and to formulate appropriate questions leading to a deeper and clearer understanding of an issue.

Judge information related to a problem. This skill requires ability to distinguish among fact, opinion, and reasoned judgment; to determine whether statements are consistent with one another and with the context from which they are taken; to identify unstated assumptions; and to recognize stereotypes, clichés, bias, propaganda, and semantic slanting.

Solve problems and draw conclusions. Included in these skills are the ability to decide whether the information provided is sufficient in quality and quantity to justify a conclusion; to identify reasonable alternatives for the solution to a problem; to test conclusions or hypotheses; and to predict probable consequences of an event, a series of events, or a policy proposal.

The ability to think critically about public issues, candidates for office, and governmental decisions is an essential attribute of good citizenship in a democratic society.

■ Basic Study Skills

The most basic skills of the history–social science fields involve obtaining information and judging its value, reaching reasoned conclusions based on evidence, and developing sound judgment.

Basic study skills are the skills that students must have in order to acquire knowledge; they are skills that make formal education possible. Most basic skills are not learned primarily through the history–social science curriculum, but some are special to this area of study. The most basic skills of the history–social science fields involve obtaining information and judging its value, reaching reasoned conclusions based on evidence, and developing sound judgment. The skills also include the ability to discuss and debate and the ability to write a well-reasoned and well-organized essay. These skills are outcomes of a well-constructed program, and they take time and practice to develop. Examples of practice include sustained reading and sustained writing.

The basic skills of history–social science include the ability to:

1. Acquire information by listening, observing, using community resources, and reading various forms of literature and primary and secondary source materials.
2. Locate, select, and organize information from written sources, such as books, periodicals, government documents, encyclopedias, and bibliographies.
3. Retrieve and analyze information by using computers, microfilm, and other electronic media.
4. Read and interpret maps, globes, models, diagrams, graphs, charts, tables, pictures, and political cartoons.
5. Understand the specialized language used in historical research and social science disciplines.
6. Organize and express ideas clearly in writing and in speaking.

Course
Descriptions

Course Descriptions

This curriculum requires an integrated and sequential development of its goals throughout the courses as well as cooperative planning among teachers.

THE course descriptions that follow provide an integrated and sequential development of the goals of this curriculum. Specific learning activities are included in these course descriptions, but they are intended to be illustrative. Imaginative teachers will create their own curricular activities to engage student participation. Specific works of literature are included in these course descriptions, but these too are meant to be illustrative. Annotated bibliographies in forthcoming editions of the *History–Social Science Model Curriculum Guide, Kindergarten Through Grade Eight* and the *Model Curriculum Standards, Grades Nine Through Twelve* will provide a broad range of readings to enrich these studies, including selections for limited-English-proficient students.

Implementation of this integrated and correlated curriculum requires cooperative planning among teachers from different subject areas, as well as school librarians, and should promote team teaching and other collaborative strategies. Teachers should draw on community resources, a wide variety of books, computer software, films, and other visual materials. In addition to presenting subjects for class discussion, teachers should provide for students' active learning through experiences such as civic participation, community service, debates, role playing, simulations, mock trials, collaborative and individual projects, preparation of local and oral histories, mapping activities, and cooperative learning.

This curriculum attempts to bridge the barriers between the related disciplines and to enable students to see the relationships and connections that exist in real life. The measure of its success will lie not only in test scores but also in the extent to which students develop empathetic insight into the life of other times and places, as well as enlightened understanding of their own time and place. The titles of courses for kindergarten through grade twelve are as follows:

Kindergarten—Learning and Working Now and Long Ago
Grade One—A Child's Place in Time and Space
Grade Two—People Who Make a Difference
Grade Three—Continuity and Change
Grade Four—California: A Changing State
Grade Five—United States History and Geography: Making a New Nation
Grade Six—World History and Geography: Ancient Civilizations
Grade Seven—World History and Geography: Medieval and Early Modern Times
Grade Eight—United States History and Geography: Growth and Conflict
Grade Nine—Elective Courses in History–Social Science
Grade Ten—World History, Culture, and Geography: The Modern World
Grade Eleven—United States History and Geography: Continuity and Change in the Twentieth Century
Grade Twelve—Principles of American Democracy (One Semester) and Economics (One Semester)

The United States and World History Courses

The curriculum departs from current practice by significantly increasing the time allocated to chronological history. The three courses in United States history (grades five, eight, and eleven) and the three courses in world history (grades six, seven, and ten) have the following characteristics:

The curriculum significantly increases the time allocated to chronological history, provides opportunities for study in depth, and emphasizes the importance of connecting with past learnings.

1. ***Beginning with grade six, each course in this series contributes to students' learning of historical chronology.*** The course in grade six emphasizes the ancient world to A.D. 500. The grade seven course continues world history through medieval and early modern times, A.D. 500—1789. The grade eight course establishes the new American nation in the context of the European Enlightenment, with which the grade seven course just concluded, and emphasizes the years 1783—1914. The grade ten course emphasizes the modern world, 1789 to the present day. The grade eleven course emphasizes United States history in the twentieth century. This interplay between world and United States history helps students recognize the global context in which their nation's history developed and allows teachers to illustrate events that were developing concurrently throughout the world.

2. ***Each course gives major emphasis to a selected historical period that students will study in depth.*** The accompanying chart illus-

Chronological Emphases for Courses in World and United States History and Geography

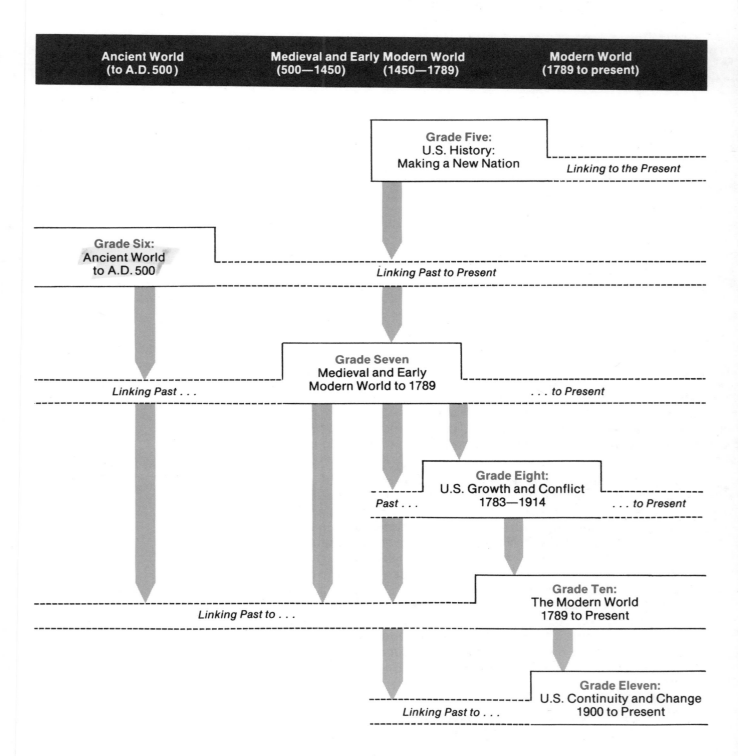

Ancient World (to A.D. 500)	Medieval and Early Modern World (500—1450) (1450—1789)	Modern World (1789 to present)

Grade Five:
U.S. History:
Making a New Nation

Linking to the Present

Grade Six:
Ancient World
to A.D. 500

Linking Past to Present

Grade Seven
Medieval and Early
Modern World to 1789

Linking Past . . .

. . . to Present

Grade Eight:
U.S. Growth and Conflict
1783—1914

Past . . .

. . . to Present

Grade Ten:
The Modern World
1789 to Present

Linking Past to . . .

Grade Eleven:
U.S. Continuity and Change
1900 to Present

Linking Past to . . .

trates the periods to be emphasized in these courses. By limiting the years to be studied in each course, this plan provides the time needed to develop these studies in depth and makes it more likely students will retain what they have learned. These outcomes cannot be achieved through the superficial treatment that results from rushing across the whole of United States or world history in one survey course.

3. ***Beginning with grade seven, each course provides for a review of learnings from earlier grades.*** Each of these courses begins with one or more review units titled, "Connecting with Past Learnings." The purpose of these units is not to cover everything that was studied in earlier years but to review selectively some essential historical antecedents of the period under study. In all of these reviews, the purpose is not to retread old ground but to develop some deeper understandings that were not possible when students were younger. These review units ensure that learnings of the ancient world will be reinforced in grades seven and ten and that learnings of the medieval and early modern worlds will be reinforced in grades eight, ten, and eleven. Learnings of our nation's seventeenth and eighteenth century beginnings are reinforced in grades eight and eleven.

4. ***Each course provides opportunities to link the past with the present.*** In the United States history sequence, the courses in grades five and eight both conclude with major units titled, "Linking Past to Present." Each of these units brings the study up to the present day by expanding on the major themes emphasized in the course. In the world history sequence, the courses in grades six and seven give recurrent attention to the contributions of the past to the modern world. In grades ten and eleven, students are brought to the present day through studies of the great changes of the twentieth century that have shaped the world in which students live.

The Primary Curriculum, Kindergarten Through Grade Three

Developmental Considerations

Beginning with kindergarten, the primary curriculum builds on the important learnings young children have already developed during infancy and their early preschool years. By the time they enter kindergarten, most children have developed important space, time, and causal understandings. These understandings connect and orient each child within his or her world. For most children, the world is not a buzzing, booming confusion, but is orderly, rule-governed, and predictive.

To extend these important spatial, temporal, and causal understandings, teachers must recognize the critical role the "home base"

The primary curriculum builds on the important learnings young children have already developed during infancy and their early preschool years and then moves outward through geography and back in time through history to link the child with people from the past.

plays for the young child. Geographic and historical forays in space and back through time must always be connected with the young child's immediate world and with the fund of meanings the child already has acquired. These primary studies, therefore, begin each year by centering first on the child's immediate present. Studies each year then move spatially outward to develop important linkages with the larger geographic and economic world. Studies each year also reach back in time to link the child with people, ordinary and extraordinary, who came before and whose stories build sensitivity and appreciation for times past and for the long continuity of human experience.

A summary of the course titles for kindergarten and grades one through three, with major subtitles, is as follows:

Kindergarten—Learning and Working Now and Long Ago
- Learning to Work Together
- Working Together: Exploring, Creating, and Communicating
- Reaching Out to Times Past

Grade One—A Child's Place in Time and Space
- Developing Social Skills and Responsibilities
- Expanding Children's Geographic and Economic Worlds
- Developing Awareness of Cultural Diversity, Now and Long Ago

Grade Two—People Who Make a Difference
- People Who Supply Our Needs
- Our Parents, Grandparents, and Ancestors from Long Ago
- People from Many Cultures, Now and Long Ago

Grade Three—Continuity and Change
- Our Local History: Discovering Our Past and Our Traditions
- Our Nation's History: Meeting People, Ordinary and Extraordinary, Through Biography, Story, Folktale, and Legend

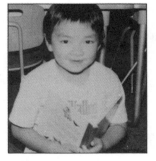

In kindergarten children learn what is necessary for good civic behavior in the classroom and in the larger society.

■ Kindergarten—
Learning and Working Now and Long Ago

In kindergarten children first begin to understand that school is a place for learning and working. Most children arrive for their first school experience eager to work and learn. Most will be working in groups for the first time. They must learn to share, to take turns, to respect the rights of others, and to take care of themselves and their own possessions. These are learnings that are necessary for good civic behavior in the classroom and in the larger society. Children can also discover how other people have learned and worked together by hearing stories of times past.

Learning to Work Together

To help children learn their way as learners, workers, and class-room participants is the purpose of this first study. In the daily life of the kindergarten, children are invited to work centers and activities, encouraged to participate, and given guidance in acquiring the complex skills involved in working with others. They must learn to share the attention of the teacher with others and learn to consider the rights of others in the use and care of classroom materials.

Such learnings will be deepened and enriched if teachers use class-room problems that inevitably arise as opportunities for critical think-ing and problem solving; for example, problems in sharing scarce resources or space with others or in planning ahead and bringing one's activity to a conclusion to be on time for the next. Children need help in analyzing problems such as these; considering why the problem arose; considering other alternatives they might have tried in coping with the problem; developing awareness of how alternative behaviors might bring different results in the ways that others in the group respond to them; and learning to appreciate behaviors and values that are consis-tent with the democratic ethic. Children must have opportunities to dis-cuss these more desirable behaviors, try them out, and examine how they lead to more harmonious and socially satisfying relationships with others.

To further support these learnings, teachers should introduce stories, fairy tales, and nursery rhymes that incorporate conflict and raise value issues that are both interesting and understandable for young children. A few examples of such stories are "Jack and the Beanstalk," "Goldilocks and the Three Bears," selections from *Aesop's Fables,* and Virginia Hamilton's *The People Could Fly*. In discussing these stories, children should identify the behavior of characters in the story, observe the effect of this behavior on others, examine why characters behaved as they did, and consider whether other choices could have changed the results. These discussions are intended to help children think through the consequences of behavior and to help them acquire those values of deliberation and individual responsibility that are consistent with the democratic ethic.

Teachers should introduce stories, fairy tales, and nursery rhymes that incorporate conflict, raise value issues, and help students to reach out to times past.

Working Together: Exploring, Creating, and Communicating

A second major goal of this kindergarten curriculum is to help chil-dren build their sense of self and self-worth through extending their understanding of the immediate world and deepening their appreciation of their own ability to explore, create, solve problems, communicate, and assume individual and group responsibilities in classroom activities.

Children should have opportunities, under the teacher's guidance, to explore the school and its environs, a new world for these children, as well as the landscape in the neighborhood, including its topography, streets, transportation systems, structures, and human activities.

Children should have opportunities to use large building blocks, wood, tools, and miniature vehicles as well as a variety of materials from a classroom box filled with imaginative and improvisational objects,

Children build their sense of self and self-worth and assume individual and group responsibilities in classroom activities.

clothing, workers' hats, and the like in order to construct real and imagined neighborhood structures. Activities in these centers carried on through group play become important beginnings of map work for young children. Children should be encouraged to build neighborhoods and landscapes and to incorporate such structures as fire stations, airports, houses, banks, hospitals, supermarkets, harbors, and transportation lines. Picture files, stories, and books should be used to deepen children's information about the places they are creating and the work that is carried on in them. In all of these activities, children should understand the importance of literacy as a means of acquiring valuable information and knowledge.

Reaching Out to Times Past

A third goal of this kindergarten curriculum is to help children take their first vicarious steps into times past. Well-selected stories can help children develop a beginning sense of historical empathy. They should consider how it might have been to live in other times and places and how their lives would have been different. They should observe different ways people lived in earlier days; for example, getting water from a well, growing their food, making their clothing, and having fun in ways that are different from those of today. They can compare themselves with children in such stories as *Daniel's Duck* by Clyde R. Bulla, *Thy Friend, Obadiah* and *The Adventures of Obadiah* by Brinton Turkle, *Becky and the Bear* by Dorothy Van Woerkom, and selected chapters from *Little House in the Big Woods* by Laura I. Wilder.

Children take their first vicarious steps into times past. Well-selected stories can help children develop a beginning sense of historical empathy.

■ Grade One—
A Child's Place in Time and Space

Children in the first grade are ready to learn more about the world they live in and about their responsibilities to other people. They begin to learn how necessary it is for people and groups to work together and how to resolve problems that get in the way of cooperation. Children's expanding sense of place and spatial relationships provides readiness for many new geographical learnings. Children also are ready to develop a deeper understanding of cultural diversity and to appreciate the many different people and ways of life that exist in the larger world that they are now beginning to explore.

Children will learn more about their responsibilities to other people, will explore their geographic and economic world, and will develop an awareness of cultural diversity through literature-enriched experiences.

Developing Social Skills and Responsibilities

Most children in the first grade willingly accept responsibility for classroom chores. With guidance, they should be building the values of responsible classroom participation throughout the school day. Their early learnings of basic civic values can be extended now by emphasizing the values of fair play and good sportsmanship, respect for the rights and opinions of others, and respect for rules by which we all must live.

Again, as in kindergarten, emphasis should be placed on having the children solve the social problems and decision-making dilemmas that naturally arise in the life of the classroom; for example, problems in sharing scarce supplies or in deciding how best to proceed on a group project (such as map making) when a dilemma arises. In using this problems approach, children will learn that problems are a normal and recurring feature of social life and that the children themselves have the capacity to examine problems, judge their possible causes, and develop more effective ways of dealing with the problems.

Beyond the problems that normally occur in classrooms, corridors, and playgrounds, teachers can also introduce value-laden problems for discussion through reading stories and fairy tales that pose dilemmas appropriate for young children. Through listening to these stories and through the discussions and role-playing activities that can follow, children will gain deeper understandings of individual responsibility and social behavior. Throughout these lessons the teacher's purpose should be to help children develop those civic values that are important in a democratic society.

Children develop civic values that are important in a democratic society.

Expanding Children's Geographic and Economic Worlds

The children's growing sense of place and spatial relationships makes possible important new geographic learnings in grade one. Unless children are new to the area, they probably already have developed a good sense of their neighborhood and the places they regularly go to shop, play, and visit with family and friends. They are now ready to develop a deeper understanding of these places and the interrelationships between these places and the other places, both near and far, that supply their needs.

Children's growing sense of place and spatial relationships makes possible important new geographic learnings.

Regions that are changing provide especially rich opportunities for the geographic and economic education of young children. In these places children can observe firsthand the changes that are occurring in the landscape, such as new shopping malls and freeways, and land-use changes that turn residential neighborhoods into commercial areas and rural areas into urban communities. Children can also analyze why these changes are happening and how these changes are affecting their families and others who live here.

To develop these geographic learnings, children need to build a three-dimensional floor or table map of their immediate geographic region. Such an activity helps develop children's observational skills; teaches the concepts of geographic scale, distance, and relative location; and clarifies for children the spatial relationships among the region's features. Small building blocks or milk cartons can be used to simulate neighborhood structures. Instant photos taken by children on teacher-conducted walks "in the field" can be taped to the front of each "building" as a quick and temporary way of establishing its identity. Street signs, signals, crosswalks, mailboxes, and model vehicles, such as delivery trucks, dumpsters, cars, and buses, can be added to represent the variety of human activities going on in this region. Throughout all these activities children should consult their textbooks, picture files, and a wide variety of books for information about these workplaces and the work people do in them.

Comparing such a floor or table map to a picture map of this same region will help children make the connections between geographic features in the field, three-dimensional models of this region, and two-dimensional pictures or symbolic maps. Children should observe that the picture-symbol map "tells the same story" as the floor model but does so at a smaller scale. They should also observe that the picture-symbol map can be hung upright without changing the spatial arrangement of these features and without altering their relationships to one another; for example, the supermarket is still north of the post office. Children must have these critical understandings if they are to read and interpret the data that maps represent. These understandings are basic to all subsequent map reading and interpretation skills.

Once children have developed an educated understanding of their neighborhood, they are ready to examine its many geographic and economic connections with the larger world. This study, therefore, moves next to the central post office through which the letters they mail to families and friends are routed for delivery here and abroad; to the trucks and railroad lines that bring products to this neighborhood for eventual sale in its stores; to an industrial region, near or far away, producing one or more needed products, such as bricks and building materials for new home construction or clothing for the stores; and to the airport or regional harbor that links this place with producers, suppliers, and families throughout the world. Children at this age level should understand that the place where they live is interconnected with the wider world.

In these studies the children should be acquiring some basic understanding of economics; for example, of the goods and services that people need and want and of the specialized work that people do to manufacture, transport, and market such goods and services.

At the same time children should be enjoying literature that brings these activities alive and that builds sensitivity toward the many people who work together to get their jobs done. Classic stories such as *Mike Mulligan and His Steam Shovel, Little Toot,* and *The Little Red Lighthouse and the Great Gray Bridge* illustrate working together, teach values, and develop empathy.

Developing Awareness of Cultural Diversity, Now and Long Ago

This unit of study focuses on many people: people from the children's own families and those of their classmates, people from other cultures, people living today, and people from long ago. Through stories of today as well as fairy tales, folktales, and legends that open the richness of the past to young children, this curriculum helps children to discover the many ways in which people, families, and cultural groups are alike as well as those ways in which they differ.

In developing this literature-enriched unit of study, teachers should draw first from the rich fund of literature from those cultures represented among the families in the classroom and school. Then, as time

Children enjoy literature that builds sensitivity toward others.

allows, teachers can introduce literature from other cultures for comparison.

Throughout this unit opportunities should be provided for children to discuss and dramatize these stories, discover their moral teachings, and analyze what these stories tell about the culture: its beliefs, customs, ceremonies, traditions, social practices, and the like. In addition, children should read stories about men and women who are heroes.

Among the literary treasures young children can enjoy are fairy tales by the Brothers Grimm; *Aesop's Fables;* Ethel J. Phelps's *Tatterhood and Other Tales,* a multicultural collection of traditional folktales in which girls are the heroes; African folktales, including Camille Yarbrough's *Cornrows*; Japanese folklore, including Yoshiko Uchida's *Magic Listening Cap* and Taro Yashima's *Umbrella;* Frances Carpenter's *Tales of a Korean Grandmother;* American folktales and hero stories, such as *John Henry: An American Legend* by Ezra J. Keats; selected American Indian tales of California, the Great Plains, and the Southwest; and Leo Politi's stories of Hispanic Los Angeles. By the end of grade one, the children should appreciate the power and pleasure of reading.

Among the literary treasures young children can enjoy are fairy tales, folktales, American Indian tales, and stories of the Southwest.

By the end of grade one, the children should appreciate the power and pleasure of reading.

■ Grade Two—
People Who Make a Difference

Children in the second grade are ready to learn about people who make a difference in their own lives and who made a difference in the past. People who make a difference in the child's world are, first, those who care for him or her; second, those who supply the goods and services that are necessary for daily life; and third, those extraordinary men and women who have made a difference in our national life and in the larger world community.

Children develop an appreciation of the many people who make a difference in their lives, those who supply their daily needs, and those who have helped make their world a better place.

People Who Supply Our Needs

This first study develops children's appreciation of the many people who work to supply their daily needs. Emphasis in this unit is given to those who supply food: people who grow and harvest food crops on wheat and vegetable farms, fruit orchards, or the banana plantations of Central America; dairy workers who supply dairy products; and processors and distributors who move the food from farm to market. In addition, students should consider the interdependence of all these people, consumers and producers, processors and distributors, in bringing these foods to market.

In visits to their local market and to a regional central market, if available, children should observe and identify the great variety of foods that workers in these markets make available to buyers on a daily basis.

Questions of where these foods come from, who produces them, and how they reach these markets give focus to this unit.

To engage children's interest and to help them develop an understanding of the complex interdependence among many workers in the food industry, teachers should guide children in creating large three-dimensional floor or table maps. Children can begin these maps with small models of the school, nearby homes, and the local market as well as the major streets, roads, freeways, or highways in the immediate neighborhood of the school. These models can be constructed of wood, small building blocks, or even milk cartons, and they can be painted with poster paints to simulate the buildings they represent. Then, by adding model structures, highways, and railroad lines as the study proceeds, children can observe the many linkages between their homes, the markets that supply their food, the places where people work to produce their food, and the transportation systems that move these products from farm to processor to market.

Picture maps and flowcharts should be introduced to help children analyze the sequences and interrelationships in all these activities. Air photos and regional maps of the immediate and the extended geographic region can be introduced to help children locate the places where these activities occur and observe how farmlands, railroads, highways, and urban markets are distributed in the geographic landscape. In the course of these geographic learnings, children should differentiate between these maps and the globe, understand and use cardinal directions, identify and distinguish between physical geographic features in the natural landscape and on maps, and read and interpret map symbols with the use of a legend.

As part of these studies, children should explore such geographic questions as the following: How does climate affect the crops a farmer can grow? Why are some areas more fertile than others? How do farmers protect their crops against untimely frosts or drought? Why is water such an important resource for farmers? How do irrigation systems work? What can happen to our food supply when any part of the total system breaks down because of a flood or natural disaster or a strike of transportation workers? What can happen to our food supply if farmlands are overused or rich farmlands are changed or rezoned for urban development?

Throughout this study children should be developing basic economic understandings of human wants and needs, scarcity and choice; the importance of specialization in work today and the economic interdependence that results; the need for exchange in the market system; and the importance of international trade as they learn about bananas from Central America or cocoa products from Ghana.

Comparative studies can be based on episodes drawn from the past—episodes, for example, that introduce young children, through stories, to the domestication of wild grasses by the early peoples of Mesopotamia; the tools and technology people invented long ago to grind their grain and bake their bread; and the important invention of the mill for grinding grain, and, much later, of refrigeration for preserv-

In the course of geographic learnings, children differentiate between maps and the globe, understand and use cardinal directions, identify and distinguish between physical geographic features in the natural landscape and on maps, and read and interpret map symbols with the use of a legend.

Children develop basic economic understandings of human wants and needs, scarcity and choice; and the importance of specialization in work today, economic interdependence, and international trade.

ing food. Specific historic dates are meaningless to children of this age, but young children can grasp the drama of humankind's great achievement in taming the wild grasses for a steady food supply and the long history of the use of bread products, along with the inventions that have made the task of producing food easier and more reliable. To place these events in historical sequence, children can differentiate between those that happened long long ago, long ago, and yesterday. Children should explore the benefits of technology in food production.

Other comparative studies can center on the foods indigenous to one or more of the cultures represented in the classroom group; the production of these foods; their use in daily diets, ceremonies, and festivals; and their enjoyment by many families in California today.

Literature should be richly used throughout these studies to bring alive the people who produce and who enjoy the fruits of all these labors. Among the literary selections to be read to children and to be dramatized by them, when appropriate, are the stories of the first Thanksgiving, *The Adventures of Johnny Appleseed,* and a wide selection of folktales, myths, legends, and stories from many cultures, Western and non-Western.

Literary selections from many cultures are read to children and are dramatized.

Our Parents, Grandparents, and Ancestors from Long Ago

To understand and appreciate the many ways that parents, grandparents, and ancestors have made a difference is the central purpose of this unit of the second grade curriculum. Another purpose is to help children develop a beginning sense of history through an approach that is understandable and interesting to children.

One way to help children understand how parents and grandparents made a difference is to have them construct a family history. A child may choose to develop a history of his or her own family, a relative's or neighbor's family, or a family from books or personal experience. In developing these activities, teachers should be sensitive to family privacy and protect the wishes of children and parents who prefer not to include their families in these activities. Where did the family come from? What was it like to live there? Who was in the family then? Do photos or letters from that time still exist? When did the family come here? How did they make the trip? Were there any adventures? Are there any family legends about the journey?

Children construct a family history.

Through children's dictation, later recorded by the teacher in individual storybooks, children might tell the story of the family's transit and its adventures getting here. The children might be invited to illustrate the family history, either painting or coloring pictures themselves or using photos (if the family agrees) to show how the family has changed over one or more generations.

Class discussions can center on the many places, groups, and nations represented among classmates. A globe and world map can be used to locate places of family origin and to study possible routes followed in getting here. Transportation methods of earlier days should be compared with those a family traveling today might use.

Members of children's families can be invited to tell about the experiences of their families. Readings from literature can be shared to help children acquire deeper insights into the cultures from which the families came; the stories, games, and festivals parents or grandparents might have enjoyed as children; the work that children as well as their families would have been expected to do; their religious practices; and the dress, manners, and morals expected of family members at that time. Comparisons can be drawn with children's lives today to discover how many of these family traditions, practices, and values have carried forward to the present and what kinds of changes have occurred.

People from Many Cultures, Now and Long Ago

In this unit of study, the children will be introduced to the many people, ordinary and extraordinary, who have contributed to their lives and "made a difference." Among the people children should meet are those men and women whose contributions can be appreciated by seven-year-olds and whose achievements have directly or indirectly touched their lives or the lives of others like themselves. Included, for example, are scientists who have found a cure for childhood diseases; scientists and inventors, such as George Washington Carver, Marie Curie, Louis Pasteur, Charles Drew, and Thomas Edison; authors, musicians, and artists whose works are great favorites of children and who have brought beauty into their lives; athletes such as Jackie Robinson who have brought pleasure to sports fans and who have become role models for young people to follow; leaders from all walks of life who have helped to solve community problems, worked for better schools, or improved living conditions and lifelong opportunities for workers, families, women, and children; and children, as well as adults, who have been honored locally for the special courage, responsibility, and concern they have displayed in contributing to the safety, welfare, and happiness of others.

Through reading and listening to biographies, children can learn about the lives of those from many cultures who have made a difference. They should conclude from their studies of this year that people matter: those we know, those who lived long ago, and those who help us even though we do not know their names.

Through reading and listening to biographies, children can learn about the lives of those from many cultures who have made a difference.

People matter: those we know, those who lived long ago, and those who help us even though we do not know their names.

Children begin to think about continuity and change in their local communities and the nation by drawing on the extraordinary people in our nation's history found in biography, story, folktale, and legend.

■ Grade Three— Continuity and Change

Although third graders are not ready for a formal study of history, they can begin to think about continuity and change in their own locality and nation. By exploring their locality and locating some of the features that were built by people who lived long ago, children can make contact with times past and with the people whose activities have left their mark on the land.

Through studies of continuity and change in their locality, children can begin to think about chronological relationships and to analyze how some things change and others remain the same. To understand changes occurring today, children should explore the ways in which their locality continues to evolve. Finally, teachers should introduce children to the great legacy of local, regional, and national traditions that provide common memories and a shared sense of peoplehood for all of us.

Our Local History: Discovering Our Past and Our Traditions

Children who have constructed a family history in grade two are now ready to think about constructing a history of the place where they live today. Children might recall how the decision of their parents or grandparents to move to this place made an important difference in their lives. They might wonder whether the people who came to this place long ago made a difference, too. Discovering who these people were, when they lived here, and how they used the land gives children a focus for this first unit.

Because throughout California the geographic setting has had important effects on where and how localities developed, children should begin their third-grade studies with the natural landscape. A field trip into the immediate environment will establish familiarity with the major natural features and landforms of this region. Field trips are especially important if children have not had an opportunity before this to explore, observe, and study firsthand their local environment. Field trips may be augmented by use of videotapes, slides, and photographs of the landscape. Teachers must evaluate carefully whether the children have a clear understanding of the mountains, valleys, hills, coastal areas, oceans, lakes, desert landscapes, and other natural features of the region. One cannot assume that the children have a knowledge of these features simply because they live near them. Experience has shown that many children have never visited these places, even when these places are not far from their homes.

An important activity for children in grade three is to build a terrain model of the topography of the local region. In doing the research for this activity, children will develop an understanding of the physical setting in which their region's history has unfolded. They will learn to differentiate between major landforms in the landscape. Once the model is completed, children can consider who the first people were who lived here, how they used the resources of this region, and in what ways they modified the natural environment.

American Indians who lived in the region should be authentically presented, including their tribal identity; their social organization and customs; the location of their villages and why they were located here; the structures they built and the relationship of these structures to the climate in this place; the methods they used to get their food, clothing, tools, and utensils and whether they traded with others for any of these things; and their art and folklore. Museums that specialize in California Indian cultures are a rich source of publications, pictures, and artifacts that can help children appreciate the daily lives and the adaptation of these cultures to the environment of the geographic region.

American Indians who lived in the region should be authentically presented by their tribal identity.

Children are now ready to consider those who came into this region and the impact each new group had on those who came before. To organize this sequence of events, children should develop a classroom time line by illustrating events and placing those illustrations in sequence with a caption under each. Depending on the local history, this sequence will include the explorers who visited here; the newcomers who settled here; the economy they established; their impact on the American Indians of this region; and their lasting marks on the landscape, including the buildings, streets, political boundaries, names, customs, and traditions that continue today; the people who have continued to come to this region; and the rich legacy of cultural traditions that newcomers brought with them.

Children should observe how their community has changed over time and also why certain features have remained the same. They should compare the kinds of transportation people used long ago, the ways in which people provided water for their growing community and farmlands, the sources of power long ago, and the kinds of work people engaged in years ago. They should discover that the changing history of their locality was, at all stages, closely related to the physical geography of this region: its topography, soil, water, mineral resources, and relative location. Children should analyze how successive groups of settlers made different uses of the land, depending on their skills, technology, and values. Children should observe how each period of settlement in their locality left its mark on the land, and they should analyze how decisions being made today also will leave their effects, good or bad, for those who will come after.

To bring earlier times alive for children, teachers should provide opportunities for them to study historical photos and to observe the changes in the ways families lived, worked, played, dressed, and traveled. Children should have opportunities to role-play being an immigrant today and long ago; discover how newcomers, including children, have earned their living, now and long ago; and analyze why such occupations have changed over time. They should observe how a given place, such as Main Street, looked long ago and how it looks today. Children can compare changes in their community with slides or picture displays provided by the teacher.

The local community newspaper, the historical society, or other community organizations often can provide photos and articles on earlier events in the region—stories and pictures that capture for children a sense of what it was really like the day the town celebrated its new school, turned out for the grand opening of its new railroad station, expanded its harbor, or celebrated a town hero. Children should have opportunities to interview "old-timers" in their community or to invite them to speak to the class to build appreciation of events seen through the eyes of those who were there. When available, old maps can be a source of wonderful discoveries: where the early rancho that once occupied this land was located; how streets were laid out in an earlier day and how many of them and their names survive today; how boundaries have changed over the years and how settlements have grown; how once-open fields have changed to dense urban development; how a river or coastline has changed in location or size because of a dam constructed upstream, a great earthquake in the past, or breakwaters that have been built to change the action of the sea.

Throughout these studies children should have continuing opportunities to enjoy the literature that brings to life the people of an earlier time. The literary selections, though not specifically written about their community, should illustrate how people lived in the past and convey the way of life of those earlier times.

Finally, in each of these studies, children should be helped to compare the past to changes under way today. Are new developments changing their community? How do people today earn their living or seek recreation? How are people working to protect their region's natural resources? How do people in this community work to influence public policy, elect their city government, and participate in resolving local issues that are important to children and their families, such as the fate of a local park earmarked for commercial use? Although children are too young to act on issues such as these, they can identify some issues that are important in their immediate community. Informed volunteers in community service or elected officials can be invited to explain why people volunteer and to describe some of the arguments on different sides of an important issue facing the community.

Children should be helped to compare the past to changes under way today and to identify some issues that are important in their immediate community.

Our Nation's History: Meeting People, Ordinary and Extraordinary, Through Biography, Story, Folktale, and Legend

To understand the common memories that create a sense of community and continuity among people, children should learn about the classic legends, folktales, tall tales, and hero stories of their community and nation. Stories such as Ingri and Edgar D'Aulaire's *Christopher Columbus,* Joan Sandin's *The Long Road to a New Land,* Thomas P. Lewis's *Clipper Ship,* Barbara Brenner's *Wagon Wheels,* Elizabeth Shub's *The White Stallion,* F. N. Monjo's *The Drinking Gourd,* and Barbara Cohen's *Molly's Pilgrim* help students to appreciate those who dared to move into unknown regions. Children should listen to biographies of the nation's heroes and of those who took the risk of new and controversial ideas and opened new opportunities for many. Such stories convey to the children valuable insights into the history of their nation and its people; they also help children to understand today's great movement of immigrants into California as a part of the continuing history of their nation.

To understand the common memories that create a sense of community and continuity among people, children should learn about the classic legends, folktales, tall tales, and hero stories of their community and nation.

Through stories and the celebration of national holidays, children should learn the meaning of the nation's holidays and the symbols that provide continuity and a sense of community across time; for example, the flag, the eagle, Uncle Sam, and the Statue of Liberty. They should learn the Pledge of Allegiance to the flag and the national songs that express American ideals, such as "America the Beautiful," the "Star Spangled Banner," and "America."

The Middle Grades Curriculum, Grades Four Through Eight

Developmental Considerations

The intellectual development of a student undergoes important qualitative changes as he or she enters the years of later childhood and early adolescence. Later childhood is a time marked by relative harmony in the inner life of the child. Intellectually, most students enter this period at the level of Piaget's "concrete operations," and they negotiate during these years their transition into the early stages of logical propositional thinking.

Students' thinking during these years becomes increasingly abstract and multidimensional. They are now able to engage in comparative analyses across multiple sets of data, reason on the basis of differences among the data, and develop and test hypotheses through deductive analysis and the "test of the new case." These are powerful analytical processes that challenge students' interest and attention, but they are skills that must be supported by a wide variety of concrete instructional aids, maps, two- and three-dimensional charts for organizing data, and time lines. With such aids students will be able to make these critical comparisons and draw valid inferences.

Because of these developing capabilities, students throughout grades four through eight can consider a far wider sweep of human affairs. They can reach back in time to study specific people and events that contributed to the evolution of their own society, its values, and its institutions. They can follow with interest the origin and development of major Western and non-Western civilizations. In all these studies, however, teachers must recognize the limitations on what students in grades four through eight can understand. Historical analyses must continue to be grounded in the lives of people and events. Specific periods of history must be given the time required to study each fully and in depth and to learn about the people and events, ordinary and extraordinary, that make these studies exciting. This emphasis on people is especially appropriate in grades four through eight, because these are the years when students are especially open and receptive to the study of people who are different from themselves.

The course titles and major subtitles for grades four through eight are as follows:

Grade Four—California: A Changing State
- The Physical Setting: California and Beyond
- Pre-Columbian Settlements and People
- Exploration and Colonial History
- Missions, Ranchos, and the Mexican War for Independence
- Gold Rush, Statehood, and the Westward Movement

Students study, through history, the origin and development of major Western and non-Western civilizations.

Historical analyses must be grounded in the lives of people and events, and specific periods of history must be studied fully and in depth.

- The Period of Rapid Population Growth, Large-Scale Agriculture, and Linkage to the Rest of the United States
- Modern California: Immigration, Technology, and Cities

Grade Five—United States History and Geography: Making a New Nation

- The Land and People Before Columbus
- Age of Exploration
- Settling the Colonies
    The Virginia Settlement
    Life in New England
    The Middle Colonies
- Settling the Trans-Appalachian West
- The War for Independence
- Life in the Young Republic
- The New Nation's Westward Expansion
- Linking Past to Present: The American People, Then and Now

Grade Six—World History and Geography: Ancient Civilizations

- Early Humankind and the Development of Human Societies
- The Beginnings of Civilization in the Near East and Africa: Mesopotamia, Egypt, and Cush
- The Foundation of Western Ideas: The Ancient Hebrews and Greeks
- West Meets East: The Early Civilizations of India and China
- East Meets West: Rome

The emphasis on people is especially appropriate in grades four through eight, because these are the years when students are especially open and receptive to the study of people who are different from themselves.

Grade Seven—World History and Geography: Medieval and Early Modern Times

- Connecting with Past Learnings: Uncovering the Remote Past
- Connecting with Past Learnings: The Fall of Rome
- Growth of Islam
- African States in the Middle Ages and Early Modern Times
- Civilizations of the Americas
- China
- Japan
- Medieval Societies: Europe and Japan
- Europe During the Renaissance, the Reformation, and the Scientific Revolution
- Early Modern Europe: The Age of Exploration to the Enlightenment
- Linking Past to Present

Grade Eight—United States History and Geography: Growth and Conflict

- Connecting with Past Learnings: Our Colonial Heritage
- Connecting with Past Learnings: A New Nation
- The Constitution of the United States
- Launching the Ship of State
- The Divergent Paths of the American People: 1800—1850
    The West
    The Northeast
    The South

- Toward a More Perfect Union: 1850—1879
- The Rise of Industrial America: 1877—1914
- Linking Past to Present

■ Grade Four—
California: A Changing State

The ethnic diversity, the economic energy of its people, and the variety of its geographical settings make California a creative focus of education.

The story of California is an important one for fourth-grade students to learn. Not only is California their home; it is a fascinating study in its own right. The ethnic diversity, the richness of its culture and multi-ethnic heritage, the economic energy of its people, and the variety of its geographical settings make this state a creative focus of education for students in the fourth grade.

The story of California begins in pre-Columbian times, in the culture of the American Indians who lived here before the first Europeans arrived.

The history of California then becomes the story of successive waves of immigrants from the sixteenth century through modern times and the enduring marks each left on the character of the state. These immigrants include (1) the Spanish explorers and the Spanish-Mexican settlers of the Mission and Rancho period who introduced European plants, agriculture, and a herding economy to the region; (2) the Americans who settled here, established California as a state, and developed its mining, industrial, and agricultural economy; (3) the Asian immigrants of the second half of the nineteenth century, who provided a new supply of labor for California's railroads, agriculture, and industry and contributed as entrepreneurs and innovators, especially in agriculture; (4) the immigrants of the first half of the twentieth century, including new arrivals from Latin America and Europe; and (5) the many immigrants arriving today from Latin America, the nations of the Pacific Basin and Europe, and the continued migration of people from other parts of the United States. Because of their early arrival in the New World, blacks have been present throughout much of California's history, contributing to the Spanish exploration of California, the Spanish-Mexican settlement of the region, and California's subsequent development throughout the nineteenth and twentieth centuries.

To bring California history and geography to life for students, teachers should emphasize its people in all their ethnic, racial, and cultural diversity. Fourth-grade students should learn about the daily lives, adventures, and accomplishments of these people and the cultural traditions and dynamic energy that have formed the state and shaped its varied landscape.

In grade four emphasis should also be placed on the regional geography of California. Students should analyze how the different regions of the state have developed through the interaction of physical characteristics and cultural forces and how the landscape of California has provided different resources to different people at different times, from the earliest era to the present.

The Physical Setting: California and Beyond

Students should locate California on the map and examine its setting on the western edge of North America, separated from the more densely settled parts of the American heartland by wide desert regions. They should learn to identify the mountain ranges, major coastal bays and natural harbors, and expansive river valleys and delta regions that are a part of the setting that has attracted settlement for tens of thousands of years.

Pre-Columbian Settlements and People

California has long been home to a significant percentage of the American Indian population. Even in pre-Columbian times, approximately 7 to 10 percent of the American Indian population lived along the coast, in the river valleys, and in the desert areas of California. Students should learn about the major language groups of the American Indians and their distribution, social organization, economic activities, legends, and beliefs. Students should become aware of the extent to which early people of California used natural settings without significantly modifying the environment.

Contemporary cities and densely settled areas frequently are located in the same areas as these early American Indian settlements, especially on the coasts where rivers meet the sea. In analyzing how geographical factors have influenced the location of settlements, then and now, students should have an opportunity to observe how the past and the present may be linked by similar dynamics.

Exploration and Colonial History

In this unit students will learn about the Spanish exploration of the New World and the colonization of New Spain. Attention should be paid to motives for colonization, especially those that brought Spanish soldiers and missionaries northward from Mexico City to Alta California. The stories of Junipero Serra, Juan Crespi, and Gaspar de Portolá should be told. The presence of black explorers and soldiers in the earliest Spanish expeditions by sea and land and the participation of Spaniards, Mexicans, and blacks in the founding of the Alta California settlements should be noted. In mapping these routes and settlements, students should observe that access to California was difficult because of the physical barriers of mountains, deserts, and ocean currents.

Missions, Ranchos, and the Mexican War for Independence

One reason for settling California was to bring Christianity to the native peoples. Students should understand the geographical factors involved in locating the missions so that they were a day's walk apart and situated along native pathways near sources of water. Presidios

Emphasis should be placed on the regional geography of California and the landscape of California as a provider of different resources to different people at different times, from the earliest era to the present.

47

were erected by the colonial governors on sites that could be defended. Cattle ranches and agricultural villages were developed around the missions and presidios. European plants, agriculture, and a herding economy were introduced to the region.

To bring the history of this period to life, teachers should emphasize the daily lives of the people who occupied the ranchos, missions, presidios, haciendas, and pueblos. Reading literature; making field trips to a mission or Early California home; singing songs; and dramatizing a rodeo, fiesta, or trading day when Yankee clipper ships arrived to trade for California hides and tallow will bring this period alive. The Mexican War for Independence should be studied and discussed. What changes did Mexico's independence from Spain bring to Alta California? By analyzing California's geography, students will see how the natural barriers and remoteness of the region influenced settlement patterns during this period.

Gold Rush, Statehood, and the Westward Movement

The Gold Rush brought many changes to California by bringing sudden wealth to the state; and by affecting its population, culture, politics, and cities.

By developing a time line, students will be able to put into chronological order four events that changed the course of California history: the establishment of the Bear Flag Republic, the Mexican-American War, the Gold Rush, and California's admission to statehood in 1850. These events should be studied, discussed, and analyzed. Students should learn how gold was discovered and how news of the discovery spread throughout the world. Reading about the travels of Jedediah Smith, James Beckwourth, John C. Fremont, and the Bidwell and Donner parties should help students appreciate the hardships of the overland journey to California. Comparisons should be made with those who took the Panama route and those who came around Cape Horn by ship. The arrivals of Asians, Latin Americans, and Europeans should be noted. To bring this period to life, students should sing the songs and read the literature of the day, including newspapers. They might dramatize a day in the goldfields and compare the life and fortunes of a gold miner with those of traders in the gold towns and merchants in San Francisco.

Students should learn about women who helped to build California during these years.

Students should consider how the Gold Rush changed California by bringing sudden wealth to the state; affecting its population, culture, and politics; and instantly transforming San Francisco from a small village in 1847 to a bustling city in 1849. On the negative side, the Gold Rush robbed many of California's earlier settlers of their land grants and property rights and caused irreparable environmental destruction through the system of hydraulic mining that was introduced in the 1850s. Students should learn about women who helped to build California during these years, such as Bernarda Ruiz and Biddy Mason. Comparisons can be made between governments during the Spanish and Mexican periods and after California became a state. California's state constitution and the government it created should be introduced.

The Period of Rapid Population Growth, Large-Scale Agriculture, and Linkage to the Rest of the United States

The years following 1850 brought important changes to California. The Pony Express, the Overland Mail Service, and the telegraph service linked California with the East. The completion of the transcontinental railroad in 1869 linked California with the rest of the nation. With the help of topographic maps, students can follow the "sledge and shovel army" of Irish workers who laid the tracks westward across the Great Plains and the legions of Chinese workers who forged eastward from Sacramento through the towering Sierra Nevada mountains, digging tunnels and building bridges with daring skill. Completion of the railroad opened a flourishing trade between the Orient and eastern cities and brought thousands of new settlers to California. Students should analyze the growing hostilities toward the large Chinese labor force in California during the 1870s that led to the Chinese Exclusion Act of 1882.

The invention of the refrigerated railroad car opened eastern markets to California fruit and produce. Students should examine the special significance of water in a state in which agricultural wealth depends on cultivating dry regions with their longer growing seasons and warmer weather. Students should examine the reclamation of California's marshlands west of the Sierra Nevada and the great engineering projects that bring water to the Central Valley and the semiarid south. Students should also examine the continuing conflicts over water rights.

As California became home to diverse groups of people, its culture reflected a mixture of influences from Mexico, the Far East and Pacific regions, and various European nations. With cultural diversity, however, came elements of tension. Students can compare the many cultural and economic contributions these diverse populations have brought to California and can make the same comparisons for California today.

Students compare the many cultural and economic contributions of diverse populations.

Modern California: Immigration, Technology, and Cities

Students in grade four should learn about the development of present-day California with its commerce, large-scale commercial agriculture, communications industry, aerospace technology, and important trade links to nations of the Pacific Basin and the world. Since the beginning of World War II, California has changed from an underdeveloped, resource-producing area to an industrial giant. Students might analyze how California's industrial development was strengthened after the war by the building of an extensive freeway system and water projects, including canals, dams, reservoirs, and power plants, to support the growing population and its need for electrical power. Students should examine the impact of these engineering projects on California's wild rivers and watersheds and the long-term consequences of California's heavy overdraft on its ground water resources.

California has changed from an underdeveloped resource-producing area to an industrial giant.

During this time California also developed a public education system, including universities and community colleges, which became a model for the nation. Students should be helped to see how good public education opens new opportunities for immigrant youth as well as native-born residents. They should analyze how California's leadership in science, the aerospace industry, agricultural research, economic development, business, and industry depends on strong public education for all.

California developed a public education system, which became a model for the nation.

Students should explore the relationship between California's economic and population growth in the twentieth century and its geographical location and environmental factors. They should look for the linkages between California's location in the Pacific Basin and the sources of recent immigration to the state. They should examine California's growing trade with nations of the Pacific Basin and analyze how California's port cities, economic development, and cultural life benefit from this trade.

This unit will conclude with an examination of some of the unresolved problems facing California today and the efforts of concerned citizens who are seeking to address these issues.

■ Grade Five—
United States History and Geography: Making a New Nation

This course for grade five presents the story of the development of the nation, with emphasis on the period up to 1850. This course focuses on one of the most remarkable stories in history: the creation of a new nation, peopled by immigrants from all parts of the globe and governed by institutions founded on the Judeo-Christian heritage, the ideals of the Enlightenment, and English traditions of self-government. This experiment was inspired by the innovative dream of building a new society, a new order for the ages, in which the promises of the Declaration of Independence would be realized.

The creation of this nation was inspired by the dream of building a new society in which the promises of the Declaration of Independence would be realized.

Wherever possible, events should be seen through the eyes of participants such as explorers, American Indians, colonists, free blacks and slaves, children, or pioneers. The narrative for the year must reflect the experiences of different racial, religious, and ethnic groups.

The Land and People Before Columbus

In this unit students examine major pre-Columbian settlements: the cliff dwellers and pueblo people of the desert Southwest; the American Indians of the Pacific Northwest; the nomadic tribes of the Great Plains; and the woodland peoples east of the Mississippi. Students should learn how these people adjusted to their natural environment; developed an economy and system of government; and expressed their culture in art, music, and dance. Students should be introduced to the rich mythology and literature of American Indian cultures.

Age of Exploration

In this unit students will concentrate on European explorers who sought trade routes, economic gain, adventure, national glory, and "the greater glory of God." Tracing the routes of these explorers on the globe should encourage discussion of the technological developments that made this age of exploration possible: the compass, the astrolabe, and seaworthy ships. Students might imagine how these explorers and their crews might have felt when they left charted seas to explore the unknown. What happened when they encountered indigenous people? How were they received when they returned home not with exotic spices and silk, but with native people, animals, plants, and even gold?

Settling the Colonies

A brief survey should be made of French, Portuguese, and Spanish colonization in the New World. Major emphasis should then be placed on the English colonies where the political values and institutions of the new nation were shaped.

Emphasis should be placed on the English colonies where the political values and institutions of the new nation were shaped.

The Virginia Settlement. In light of the failure of its predecessors, the settlement of Jamestown was a risky venture. The struggle to survive was led by Captain John Smith, who refused food to laggards. He directed the digging of wells, the planting of crops, and the construction of shelter. The economy at Jamestown was perilous until John Rolfe introduced West Indian tobacco, which became the foundation of the plantation economy. Students can explore the implications of this event. Why was tobacco grown on large plantations? What type of work force was required? What was an indentured servant? What was the social life of the plantation?

The settlement of Jamestown was a risky venture.

Students will learn of the first Africans who were brought to the colony in 1619. During the seventeenth century some Africans were indentured, some were enslaved, and some were free. Changing economic conditions increasingly caused tobacco planters to turn to slavery as a major source of reliable though costly labor. Map study will clarify the eighteenth century Atlantic trade that linked Africa, the West Indies, the British colonies, and Europe. Students should use their growing sense of historical empathy to imagine how these young men and women felt, having been stolen from their families, carried across the ocean in a brutal voyage to a strange land, and then sold into bondage. This is an appropriate time to reflect on the meaning of slavery both as a legal institution and as an extreme violation of human rights. Original documents such as brief excerpts from slave narratives and from southern statutes and laws concerning the treatment of slaves should be used.

In their study of Virginia, students should understand the importance of the House of Burgesses as the first representative assembly in the colonies. Who was allowed to vote? Who was excluded? They also should learn the meaning of the *established church*.

Life in New England. New England provided a dramatic contrast with the southern colonies. This was a region settled by two groups of Puritans who sought a life based on their religious beliefs: the separatist Pilgrims who broke with the Church of England and the Puritans who sought to reform the church from within.

New England provided a dramatic contrast with the southern colonies.

The story of the Pilgrims begins with their flight from England in search of religious freedom, their temporary haven in the Netherlands, and their voyage to the New World aboard the Mayflower. The Pilgrims' religious beliefs and their persecution by the Church of England should be fully discussed. After an arduous trip they joined in signing the Mayflower Compact, a first step toward self-government. In keeping with the times, women were not asked to sign. Why not? This is an opportunity to discuss what self-government means and to reflect on the importance of the right to vote.

Students discuss what self-government means and reflect on the importance of the right to vote.

Life in the new land was hard, and at first the Indians aided the settlers. In time the Pilgrim colonies became well established despite bloody conflicts with the indigenous people. Students should learn about the political, religious, economic, and social life of the colonies. They should be helped to envision their simple homes and the rigors of each day. They should analyze the work of men, women, and children and see how butter was churned, cloth was dyed, and soap and candles were made; they should see the hornbooks from which children learned their ABCs. By dramatizing a day in a colonial school, students will gain an understanding of the children's lives in this period, the way they learned, and disciplinary practices of that time.

The story of the Puritans is equally important in light of their enduring influence on American literature, education, and attitudes toward life and work. Inspired by their religious zeal, Puritans sought to establish a new Zion, "a city upon a hill," where they might live out their religious ideals. Led by John Winthrop, they founded the city of Boston and within ten years had opened Harvard College and the first common school in Massachusetts. They valued hard work, social obligation, simple living, and self-governing congregations. Their religious views shaped their way of life, their clothing, their laws, their forms of punishment, their educational practices, and their institutions of self-government. While they came in pursuit of freedom of religion, however, the Puritans were intolerant of dissent. The stories of Anne Hutchinson and Roger Williams are milestones in the development of religious freedom in Connecticut and Rhode Island.

The Middle Colonies. The colonies of New Amsterdam, New Jersey, Pennsylvania, Maryland, and Delaware provided havens for a wide variety of ethnic, linguistic, and religious groups, including English, Dutch, Swedish, German, Irish, Scottish, Catholic, and Jewish settlers. Special attention should be paid to Pennsylvania, where William Penn founded a Quaker colony that practiced religious freedom and representative government. Industrious farmers, fur traders, skilled craftspersons, merchants, bankers, shipbuilders, and overseas traders made the colony prosperous.

The middle colonies provided havens for a wide variety of ethnic, linguistic, and religious groups.

Geographic factors enabled the middle colonies to thrive and contributed to the development of New York and Philadelphia as busy seaports. Excerpts from Benjamin Franklin's *Autobiography* and *Poor Richard's Almanac,* his story, "The Whistle," as well as Margaret Cousins's *Ben Franklin of Old Philadelphia* should give students a sense of these times.

Settling the Trans-Appalachian West

Biographies of Daniel Boone will introduce children to English forays into the French territory west of the Appalachian Mountains and to the French and Indian War in which Boone served. Students should learn about the importance of the war in shattering French power in North America. The English attempt to reserve the land west of the Appalachians for the inland Indian nations failed. Students should follow the exploits of pathfinders such as Daniel Boone and read about the settlers who followed his trail over the Cumberland Gap into Kentucky. They should consider the viewpoint of the American Indians who occupied these same lands and read about the conflicts between the Indians and Kentucky settlers that followed the outbreak of the Revolutionary War. This frontier period is rich in biographies, tall tales, legends, songs, and handicrafts, which help to make this period vivid for students.

This frontier period is rich in biographies and tall tales, legends, songs, and handicrafts.

The War for Independence

Events leading to the Revolutionary War should be presented as a dramatic story. Each effort by the British to impose their will on the colonies resulted in a strong counterreaction and a growing spirit of independence. Students should become familiar with the Stamp Act of 1765 and the outraged colonial reaction to it; the Townshend Acts that again stirred protest and led to the Boston Massacre; and the tax on tea that provoked the Boston Tea Party. Parliament's efforts to repress dissent led to the first Continental Congress of 1774 and the Committees of Correspondence that established communication among the colonies and developed a national consciousness.

Events leading to the Revolutionary War present a dramatic story from the Declaration of Independence to victory.

In discussing the conflict, students should read excerpts from speeches in the Parliament by William Pitt and Edmund Burke, whose pleas for moderation were ignored. Students should realize that some colonists remained loyal to King George III. Major events in the Revolution should be vividly described, including the battles of Bunker Hill, Lexington, and Concord; the selection of George Washington to command the army; and Patrick Henry's famous appeal to his fellow legislators to support the fight. The role of free blacks in the battles of the American Revolution should be considered. Students should learn about Abigail Adams, Molly Pitcher, Nathan Hale, and Benedict Arnold; and they should understand the significance of the events at Valley Forge, the alliance with France, and the final battle at Yorktown.

As the war began, young Thomas Jefferson drafted the Declaration of Independence with its idealistic statements that all men are created equal and that governments derive their just power from the consent of the governed. Students should understand the courage required of those who signed this document because they risked their lives and property. Many Americans realized for the first time the contradiction between these ideals and slavery. After the war the northeastern and middle Atlantic states abolished slavery, and the Northwest Ordinance of 1787 banned slavery from the new territories north of the Ohio River. The antislavery movement did not, however, significantly affect the South, where nine out of ten American slaves lived.

To deepen their understanding of this period, students should read biographies of leaders such as George Washington, Thomas Jefferson, and Benjamin Franklin; they should also read Ralph Waldo Emerson's "Concord Hymn," Henry Wadsworth Longfellow's "Paul Revere's Ride," and fine historical fiction such as Esther Forbes's *Johnny Tremain,* Patricia Clapp's *I'm Deborah Sampson: A Soldier in the War of the Revolution,* and James L. Collier's *My Brother Sam Is Dead.*

Life in the Young Republic

In this unit students examine the daily lives of those who built the young republic under the new Constitution. Between 1789 and 1850, new waves of immigrants arrived from Europe, especially English, Scots-Irish, Irish, and Germans. Traveling by overland wagons, canals, flatboats, and steamboats, these newcomers advanced into the fertile Ohio and Mississippi valleys and through the Cumberland Gap to the South. Students should sing the songs of the boatmen and pioneers and read the tall tales of legendary figures such as Mike Fink and Paul Bunyan. They should read Ingri and Edgar D'Aulaire's *Abraham Lincoln,* which describes his boyhood in Illinois during this period, and books such as Enid Meadowcroft's *By Wagon and Flatboat.* They should learn about the Louisiana Purchase and the expeditions of Lewis and Clark and of John C. Fremont.

Students should learn about the resistance of American Indian tribes to encroachments by settlers and about the government's policy of Indian removal to lands west of the Mississippi. Students can study these events by reading the biographies of leaders such as Chief Tecumseh of the Shawnee, Chief John Ross of the Cherokee tribe, and Chief Osceola of the Seminole tribe, as well as the tragic story of the Cherokees' "Trail of Tears."

The New Nation's Westward Expansion

In this unit students examine the advance of pioneer settlements beyond the Mississippi. The flow of migration westward included grizzled fur traders and mountain men, settlers heading for Texas, Mormon families on their way to the new Zion in Utah, midwestern farmers moving to western Oregon's fertile valleys, and forty-niners bound for the Mother Lode region of California. Not to be forgotten are the whalers, New England sailors engaged in the hide and tallow trade with California, and sea traders in furs (sea otter and seal) who plied their clipper ships around Cape Horn and westward to the Pacific.

This is a period rich with folk songs and sea chanteys, folklore, tall tales, and the journals and diaries that bring this period to life. Students might dramatize the experience of moving west to Oregon by wagon train. Excerpts from Francis Parkman's *The Oregon Trail* and from children's literature will help the children understand how the expeditions were organized, how a trail was scouted, where the trail ran, and what physical dangers the pioneers faced: hostile Indians, raging rivers, parched deserts, sandstorms and snowstorms, and lack of water or medicine.

Students should compare this trail with the California overland trail, the trail to Santa Fe, and the trail to Texas, comparing each time the purpose of the journey; where the trail ran; the influence of geographic terrain, rivers, vegetation, and climate; and life in the territories at the end of these trails. Students should compare these westward migrations with the continuing northward migrations of Mexican settlers into these great Mexican territories of the West and the Southwest. While learning about life on the trail, students should discuss the reactions of the American Indians to the increasing migration and the reasons for their growing concern.

Pioneer women played varied roles in coping with the rigors of daily life on the frontier. Biographies, journals, and diaries disclose the strength and resourcefulness of pioneer women who helped to farm the land and worked as missionaries, teachers, and entrepreneurs. Many slave women gained their freedom in the West. In recognition of the new status that western women achieved, Wyoming in 1869 became the first state to grant suffrage to women.

Maps should be used to explain how and when California, Texas, and other western lands became part of the United States. Settlement was followed by battles for independence. The war with Mexico led to cession of these territories, which then became states. These events provide important opportunities to focus on the Hispanic people of California and the Southwest, on the effects of these events on their lives, and on their distinctive contributions to American culture. Students should also learn how the Oregon boundary conflict was settled by negotiation with England and how that territory became a state.

Students should compare the westward migrations of U.S. pioneers with the northward migrations of Mexican settlers into the Mexican territories of the West and the Southwest.

Linking Past to Present: The American People, Then and Now

In this unit students examine the contributions of the different groups that built the American nation and, in the process, became a new people. Students should understand that we are a people of many races, many religions, and many different national origins and that we live under a common governmental system. While this unit does not include a formal study of the Civil War, students should realize how and when slavery was brought to an end in the United States. They should also learn about the significant contributions that black men and women made to the economic, political, and cultural development of the nation, including its music, literature, art, science, medicine, technology, and scholarship.

Students should learn about the successive waves of new immigration over the years from 1850 until today. Each wave brought new people, new skills, and new cultural contributions to the development of the nation. Immigrants came from Ireland, Germany, Sweden, Norway, Italy, Russia, Poland, Hungary, China, Japan, the Philippines, the West Indies, Mexico, Greece, India, Cuba, and eventually from every corner of the globe. Immigrants farmed the plains, introduced new arts and crafts, built the railroads, developed the great southwestern mines, manned the construction industry and the steel industry, fueled the

The American people, then and now, are a people of many races, many religions, and many national origins who live under a common government.

nation's industrial growth, wrote great literature and music, produced brilliant scientists, created the entertainment industry, and provided human resources to transform the nation's economic, cultural, and social life. Students should identify the immigrants' countries of origin and locate the regions of the nation where they settled.

To understand the human side of the great drama of migration, students should read literature such as Russell Freedman's *Immigrant Kids*, Marietta Moskin's *Waiting for Mama*, Marilyn Sachs's *Call Me Ruth*, Karen Branson's *Streets of Gold*, Leonard Fisher's *Across the Sea from Galway*, and Charlene Talbot's *An Orphan for Nebraska*. They should see similar dramas re-created in the lives of recent immigrants, including Ann N. Clark's *To Stand Against the Wind*, the story of Vietnamese immigrants to America.

The newcomers often encountered discrimination because of their race, religion, or cultural traditions. They often faced hardships as they learned the new language and adjusted to a new way of life; but even more often they found the opportunity to make a new life in a land where ability and hard work enabled them to get ahead.

To understand the continuing attraction of immigrants to the United States, students should become familiar with the tenets of the American creed by discussing the meaning of key phrases in the Declaration of Independence, the Constitution, and the Bill of Rights. Students should read Emma Lazarus's poem, "The New Colossus," which is attached to the Statue of Liberty, and consider the meaning of symbols such as the statue and the phrase, *e pluribus unum*.

After a year of studying American history, students should be able to reflect on the ethical content of the nation's principles and on America's promise to its citizens—the promise of a democratic government in which the rights of the individual are protected by the government, by a free press, and by an informed public. America's ideals are closely related to the nature of American society. We are strong because we are united in a pluralistic society of many races, cultures, and ethnic groups; we have built a great nation because we have learned to live in peace with each other, respecting each other's right to be different and supporting each other as members of a common community.

Students understand that the American creed calls on them to safeguard their freedoms and those of their neighbors, to value the nation's diversity, to work for change within the framework of law, and to do their part as citizens in contributing to the welfare of their community.

Students should understand that the American creed calls on them to safeguard their freedoms and those of their neighbors, to value the nation's diversity, to work for change within the framework of law, and to do their part as citizens in contributing to the welfare of their community. To gain these understandings, students might interview elected public officials, invite volunteers from community organizations to talk about the work they do, and develop projects that can be helpful to others in their school and community. Such projects might include visits to senior citizens' centers and working on school and community beautification projects.

Throughout these activities, students should reflect on the importance of living up to the nation's ideals and of participating in the unfinished struggle to make these principles and ideals a reality for all.

■ Grade Six—
World History
and Geography:
Ancient Civilizations

In the sixth-grade curriculum, students learn about those people and events that ushered in the dawn of major Western and non-Western civilizations. Included are the early societies of the Near East and Africa, the ancient Hebrew civilization, Greece, Rome, and the classical civilizations of India and of China.

In studying the ancient world, students should come to appreciate the special significance of geographic place in the development of the human story. They should acquire a sense of the everyday life of the people; their problems and accomplishments; their relationships to the developing social, economic, and political structures of their society; the tools and technology they developed; the art they created; the architecture they lived with; the literature produced by their finest poets, narrators, and writers; their explanations for natural phenomena; and the ideas they developed that helped transform their world. In studying each ancient society, students should examine the role of women and the presence or absence of slavery.

Among the major figures whom students should come to know are those who helped to establish these early societies and their codes of ethics, justice, and their rule of law, such as Hammurabi, Abraham, Moses, David, Pericles, and Asoka; those who extended these early empires and carried their influence into much of the ancient world, including Alexander the Great, Julius Caesar, and Augustus Caesar; and those whose ideas and teachings became enduring influences in Western and non-Western thought, especially Socrates, Jesus, Buddha, and Confucius. For all these societies, emphasis should be placed on those major contributions, achievements, and belief systems that have endured across the centuries to the present day.

Early Humankind and the Development of Human Societies

This unit should develop the students' awareness of prehistoric people's chronological place on the historical time line. Attention should be given to paleontological discoveries in East Africa by Donald Johanson, Thomas Gray, and Mary Leakey, supporting the belief that ancestors of present-day humans lived in these regions between 2.5 and 3 million years ago. Studies of the Old Stone Age (Paleolithic), Middle Stone Age (Mesolithic), and New Stone Age (Neolithic) should provide students with an understanding of the interaction between the environment and the developing life-styles of prehistoric peoples as they moved from hunter-gatherers to food producers. These studies also should focus on early peoples' attempts to explain the universe through cave art

A study of ancient societies of the Near East and Africa, the ancient Hebrew civilization, Greece, Rome, and the classical civilizations of India and China introduces students to the people and events at the dawn of major Western and non-Western civilizations.

Students develop an awareness of prehistoric people's chronological place on the historical time line.

and elemental forms of religion; the development of stone tools from simple to complex to metal; and the development of language as a medium for transmitting and accumulating knowledge.

The Beginnings of Civilization in the Near East and Africa: Mesopotamia, Egypt, and Kush

Civilization begins in the Near East and Africa.

In this unit students learn about the peoples of Mesopotamia, with an emphasis on the Sumerians, their early settlements in the fertile crescent between the Tigris and Euphrates rivers and the major events marking their sojourn: the spread of their agricultural villages by 4000 B.C. to lower Mesopotamia; their technological and social accomplishments, including invention of the wheel, plow, and irrigation systems; their systems of cuneiform writing, of measurement, and of law; and the developing social, economic, and political systems that these accomplishments made possible.

Moving next to ancient Egypt, the teacher introduces students briefly to the early reign of Khufu and then moves to an emphasis on the New Kingdom in the reign of Queen Hatshepsut. The New Kingdom was a time when Egyptian art and architecture flourished, and trade extended Egyptian influence throughout the Middle East. Attention should be given to the daily lives of farmers, tradespeople, architects, artists, scribes, women, and children; and to the great trading expeditions and building activities of that time. Geographic learnings include the importance of the Nile to Egypt's development and of irrigation practices that are still in use.

This unit concludes with Africa's oldest interior empire, the Kingdom of Kush, which conquered Egypt in 751 B.C. and established the twenty-fifth dynasty of pharaohs. Conquered in turn by the Assyrians, the kings of Kush reestablished their capital farther south. Students should be introduced to the culture that developed there, including the development of iron agricultural tools and weapons; an alphabet; and a profitable trade that extended to Arabia, India, sub-Saharan Africa, and possibly China.

The Foundation of Western Ideas: The Ancient Hebrews and Greeks

The roots of Western civilization can be found in the enduring contributions of the ancient Hebrews to Western ethical and religious thought.

The roots of Western civilization can be found in the enduring contributions of the ancient Hebrews to Western ethical and religious thought and literature, most notably by the Old Testament. To understand these traditions, students should read and discuss Biblical literature that is part of the literary heritage and ethical teachings of Western civilization; for example, stories about the Creation, Noah, the Tower of Babel, Abraham, the Exodus, the Ten Commandments, Ruth and Naomi, David, and Daniel and the Lion's Den; selections from the Psalms and Proverbs; and the Hebrew people's concepts of wisdom, righteousness, law, and justice.

In studying the civilization of the ancient Greeks, students learn of the early democratic forms of government; the dawn of rational thought expressed in Greek philosophy, mathematics, science, and history; and the enduring cultural contributions of Greek art, architecture, drama, and poetry.

In this unit students will learn about the Greek polis (city-state); the rise of Athens; the transition from tyranny and oligarchy to an early form of democracy; the importance of the great fleet of Athens and its location at the crossroads of the ancient world; the rivalry between Athens and Sparta, culminating in the Peloponnesian War; the Macedonian conquests under Alexander the Great, spreading Hellenistic culture throughout the Mediterranean and Middle Eastern worlds; and the fall of Greece to Rome. Attention should be paid to the daily life of women and children in Athens and Sparta, the games and sports of the Olympiad, the education of youth, and the trial of Socrates. Particular emphasis should be placed on reading and discussing the rich myths and Homeric literature that have deeply influenced Western art, drama, and literature.

West Meets East: The Early Civilizations of India and China

Alexander the Great's conquest of Persia and its territories provides the bridge to a study of the great Eastern civilization of India. Students should understand that the culture Alexander encountered in 327 to 325 B.C. was not the first civilization of this region. Over a thousand years earlier, a great civilization had developed in the Indus River Valley, reached its zenith, and collapsed. Succeeding waves of Aryan nomads from the north spread their influence across the Punjab and Ganges plains and contributed to the rise of a civilization rich in its aesthetic culture (architecture, sculpture, painting, dance, and music) and in its intellectual traditions (Arabic numbers, the zero, medical tradition, and metallurgy).

Students should be introduced to one of the major religious traditions of India: Buddhism, a great civilizing force that emerged in the sixth century B.C. in the life and moral teachings of "The Buddha" or Siddhartha Gautama. Through the story of Buddha's life, his Hindu background, and his search for enlightenment, students can be introduced to Buddha's central beliefs and moral teachings: unselfishness (returning good for evil); compassion for the suffering of others; tolerance and nonviolence; and the prohibition of lying, stealing, killing, finding fault with others, and gossiping.

Students learn about the major religions and philosophies of India and China as part of these early civilizations.

Students also should learn about Asoka, the great philosopher-king who unified almost all of India, renounced violence as a national policy, and established Buddhism as the state religion.

The northward spread of Buddhism in the first century A.D. provides students with a bridge to a study of China during the Han Dynasty (206 B.C. to A.D. 220). Students should be helped to understand that the roots of this great civilization go far back into ancient times when Shang society (the "molders" of China) first emerged around 1500 B.C. in the Huang-Ho Valley and established the Chinese language and a highly developed technique of working with bronze.

During succeeding centuries China grew by conquering the barbarians on its borders and absorbing the lands of these barbaric people as frontier states within Chinese society. By the sixth century B.C., the balance of power between the princes of these newer states and the old imperial centers of central China had broken down, plunging China into political chaos and war. It was during this time, when traditional values were neglected and government was in disarray, that Confucius lived and wrote. He tried to make sense of a troubled world and proposed ways in which individuals and society could achieve goodness. The good person in Confucius's teaching practiced moderation in conduct and emotion, kept one's promises, learned the traditional ways, respected one's elders, improved oneself through education, and avoided people who were not good. The highest virtue for a gentleman, Confucius taught, was to govern. Attention should be paid to the role of women in Confucian society.

In 206 B.C. the Han Dynasty reunited China, made Confucian teachings official, and placed governmental administration in the hands of the educated Confucian civil service. Attention should be paid to the lives of ordinary people and the educated classes during this time of stability and prosperity. Confucian filial piety and family ties strengthened the social structure of Han society. Art, literature, and learning flourished. Agriculture, trade, and manufacturing thrived. Map study should help students analyze the growing trade and cultural interchange between China, India, and Rome at this time. The great caravan or "Silk Road" that linked China and the Middle East was in operation by the first century B.C. By the second century A.D., the various legs of the sea journey that linked China, Malaya, South India, and Egypt were completed, connecting the Far East with the Mediterranean world and Rome in one great commercial network.

East Meets West: Rome

The land and sea routes of the China trade provide students with a bridge for a return to the Mediterranean world and the study of imperial Rome. Students should learn about everyday life in Roman society, including slavery, social conflict, and the rule of Roman law. They should learn about the emergence of the Roman Republic and the spread of the Roman Empire; and about Julius Caesar, his conquests, and his assassination in 44 B.C. They also should learn of the reign of Augustus, the "Pax Romana," and the eventual division of the Roman Empire: Rome in the West and the rising Byzantine Empire in the East.

Students should learn about the rise and spread of Christianity throughout the Mediterranean world and of its origins in the life and teachings of Jesus.

Students should learn about the rise and spread of Christianity throughout the Mediterranean world and of its origins in the life and teachings of Jesus; Roman efforts to suppress Christianity; the consequences of Constantine's acceptance of Christianity (A.D. 313) and its subsequent establishment by Theodosius I as the official religion of the empire. Through selections from Biblical literature, such as the Sermon on the Mount and the parables of the Good Samaritan, the lost sheep, and the Prodigal Son, the students will learn about those teachings of Jesus that advocate compassion, justice, and love for others. To understand why the Romans thought Christianity posed a threat, students can read Paul's letter to Philemon, a letter whose moral teachings on slavery challenged by persuasion the social order and institutions of Rome.

Finally, students should compare Roman contributions in art, architecture, engineering, political thought, religion, and philosophy with those of the earlier Greeks and consider the influence of both cultures on Western civilization and on our lives today.

Throughout these grade six studies, students should be engaged in higher levels of critical thinking. They should consider, for example, why these societies developed where they did (the critical geographic relationships between site, resources, and settlement exemplified in the river valley settlements of Mesopotamia, Egypt, India, and China); why societies rose to dominance at particular times in the ancient world (the importance of "relative location" in the case of ancient Greece, for example); and why great civilizations fell, including the collapse of the Indus civilization of India, the decline of Egypt in the years of the later empire, and the fall of Greece to Rome.

Students should examine factors of continuity and change across time in the development of these civilizations, observing how major beliefs, social organization, and technological developments of an earlier era were carried through the centuries and have contributed to our own life.

Students should examine factors of continuity and change across time in the development of these early civilizations and note how they have contributed to our way of life.

Students should engage in comparative analyses across time and across cultures. They should compare, for example, the factors contributing to the evolution of ancient societies across the whole of the ancient world; the evolution of language and its written forms in Mesopotamia, Egypt, and China; and the origins of major religions and ethical belief systems that unified cultures and defined the good and right way to live. To support their analyses, students should develop mathematically accurate time lines that place events in chronological order and support comparative analyses of events simultaneously occurring in different cultural areas of the world.

Students should be engaged in mapping activities that support their analyses of where these societies first developed, the course of their spatial development over time, and their spatial interactions illustrated in the geographic movement of ideas, religious beliefs, economic trade, and military expansion throughout the ancient world.

In linking past to present, students learn to appreciate the continuity of human experience, the debt we owe to those before us who established the foundations of modern civilizations, and the responsibilities we owe to those who will come after us.

To make these studies relevant for today, students should develop appreciation of the continuity of human experience, the great debt we owe to those who came before us and established the foundations on which modern civilizations rest, and the responsibilities we owe to those who will come after us.

■ Grade Seven—
World History and Geography: Medieval and Early Modern Times

The study of world history and geography continues this year with an examination of

A review unit on the ancient world begins with a study of the ways archaeologists and historians uncover the past.

The sequence of these units is both historical, advancing across the years A.D. 500—1789, and geographic, advancing across the major continents of the earth.

Students will observe that historians and archaeologists work as detectives by formulating appropriate questions and drawing conclusions from evidence.

social, cultural, and technological change during the period A.D. 500—1789. A review unit on the ancient world begins with a study of the ways archaeologists and historians uncover the past. Then, with the fall of Rome, this study moves to Islam, a rising force in the medieval world; follows the spread of Islam through Africa; crosses the Atlantic to observe the rise of the Mayan, Incan, and Aztec civilizations; moves westward to compare the civilizations of China and Japan during the Middle Ages; returns to a comparative study of Europe during the High Middle Ages; and concludes with the turbulent age of the Renaissance, Reformation, and Scientific Revolution that ushered in the Enlightenment and the modern world.

The sequence of these units is both *historical,* advancing across the years A.D. 500—1789, and *geographic,* advancing across the major continents of the earth. The units are focused on the great civilizations that were developing concurrently over these years. By developing world maps and time lines, students can locate these cultures in time and in place, compare events that were developing concurrently in the world, and observe the transmission of ideas, beliefs, scientific developments, and economic trade throughout this important period of history.

Connecting with Past Learnings: Uncovering the Remote Past

In the first review unit of this course, the students address this question: How do we know about the past? They will see that archaeologists develop their theories by looking for clues in the legends, artifacts, and fossils left behind by ancient peoples. For more recent periods, historians use written records as well as material culture to find out what happened in the past. Through examples, students will observe that historians and archaeologists work as detectives by formulating appropriate questions and drawing conclusions from available evidence, to try to reconstruct past societies and cultures; their social structure and family life; their political and economic systems; and their language, art, architecture, beliefs, and values. Students will also learn that new discoveries by archaeologists and historians change our view of the past. The process of reconstructing the past requires knowledge, an open mind, and critical thinking.

Connecting with Past Learnings: The Fall of Rome

This second unit builds on the sixth-grade study of Roman civilization. Students should develop a map of the Roman Empire at its height, review briefly the reign of Augustus, and consider the reasons for Rome's fall to invading Germanic tribes with attention to the role of Clovis, a Christian Frank.

To help students relate this remote historical period to the present, teachers should emphasize the lasting contributions of Roman civilization, especially in the areas of law, language, technology, and the transmission of the Christian religion to the West. By learning that the law codes of most Latin countries are still based on Roman law, students will appreciate the continuing importance of Roman law and justice.

Critical thinking skills can be developed by students as they compare citizens' civic duties as taught by Roman Stoic philosophers with citizens' civic responsibilities in America today. Such skills also can be developed by comparing modern-day public works, architecture, and technology with those of the Roman Empire.

Growth of Islam

In this unit students examine the rise of Islam as a religion and as a civilization. Attention should be given to the historic events of A.D. 636—651 when Arab armies reunited the ancient Middle East. Students should analyze the geographic and economic significance of the trade routes between Asia and Europe that were used by Arab merchants. They should consider the importance of a common literary language (Arabic) and religion (Islamic) in unifying the many ethnic groups of this region. The religious ideas of Mohammed, the founder of Islam, should be discussed both for their ethical teachings and as a way of life. Mohammed should be seen as a major historical figure who helped establish the Islamic way of life, its code of ethics and justice, and its rule of law. Students should examine the position of Christians and Jews in the Islamic world who, as "People of the Book," were allowed to practice their religious beliefs. Contributions of Islamic scholars, including mathematicians, scientists, geographers, astronomers, and physicians from many ethnic groups, should be emphasized and their relationship to Greek thought acknowledged. Scholars at Baghdad and Córdoba, the two great centers of Muslim learning, helped to preserve much of the learning of the ancient world; and, by the end of the ninth century, they added important new discoveries of their own in mathematics, medicine, geography, history, and science. Attention should be paid to the flowering of Jewish civilization in Córdoba, where poets, philosophers, and scholars established a vibrant culture.

In time the influence of Greek rationalism waned, and religious mysticism came to dominate orthodox Islamic thought. In this intellectual climate, poetry and literature flourished. Students can be introduced to these achievements through selections from *The Thousand and One Nights* (Arabic) and the poetry of Omar Khayyam, a Sufi mystic (Persian).

Islam spread to Turkey, where, in the fourteenth century, the Ottoman Turks began gradually to absorb other Turkish tribes and to establish control over most of Asia Minor. In 1453 they captured Constantinople, the seat of the Byzantine Empire, and expanded into Christian Europe until nearly 1700. In studying the social structure of the Ottoman Empire, students should give attention to the role of women; the privileges of its conquered peoples; slavery; the political system; and the legal code. Analysis should be made of the geographic conditions that facilitated the expansion of Islam through the Middle East, through North and sub-Saharan Africa, to Spain, and east through Persia to India and Indonesia, with influences that persist in these regions to the present day.

Islam is examined as a religion and as a civilization whose influence continues to the present day in the areas it touched in the early centuries.

African States in the Middle Ages and Early Modern Times

This unit begins with a geographic survey of sub-Saharan Africa and the landforms, climate, vegetation, rivers, and resources associated with its major geographic regions.

Students analyze the importance of an iron technology and of geographic location and trade in the development of the sub-Saharan empires.

Students should analyze the importance of an iron technology and of geographic location and trade in the development of the sub-Saharan empires of Ghana and Mali. Both became states of great wealth— Ghana, by controlling the trade in gold from the south; and Mali, by controlling both the southern trade in gold and the northern trade in salt. Both kingdoms exercised commercial, cultural, and political power over a large part of Africa.

The Muslim conquest of Ghana ended in destruction of the kingdom (1076). Mali's rulers, on the other hand, converted to Islam. Under Islamic rule, the nation achieved recognition as a major power. Its leading city, Timbuktu, with its university became known throughout the Muslim world as a center of learning, a tradition that lasted through Mali's conquest by Songhay in the fourteenth century and Songhay's fall two centuries later to Moroccan invaders.

Civilizations of the Americas

Accomplishments of the Mayan, Aztec, and Incan civilizations are explored in both historical and geographic perspectives.

In this unit students are introduced to three great civilizations of Middle and South America: the Mayans, Aztecs, and Incas. By developing maps and time lines, students should be able to place these cultures in geographic and historical perspective. With the development of maize agriculture around 2000 B.C., foundations were laid for cultural advances in these regions. Mayan civilization achieved its Classic Age about the time the Greco-Roman civilization collapsed. The great cultural advance that began in Peru around 1000 B.C. culminated in the Imperial Incan civilization of the fourteenth century A.D. The Aztec civilization, which incorporated the achievements of its conquered neighbors, reached its height by the sixteenth century A.D.

The accomplishments of these civilizations should be explored: the Mayans for their noble architecture, calendar, pictographic writing, and astronomy; the Incas for their excellence in engineering and administration; and the Aztecs for their massive temple architecture and Aztec calendar. Historical and archaeological records should help students understand the daily lives and beliefs of these people.

China

Students examine Chinese culture and society during the Middle Ages, including the important contributions of Confucian thought.

In this unit students examine Chinese culture and society during the Middle Ages, a period that saw the remarkable development in China of great cities; construction of large seagoing vessels; and great technological progress, including the invention of the compass, gunpowder, and printing. Important economic changes during the T'ang Dynasty (A.D. 618—906) established a "modern" form of Chinese society that lasted well into the twentieth century. Students should analyze the economic foundations of this society in the conversion of the jungle regions of the Yangtze Valley into productive rice paddies. Elaborate irrigation systems and canals supported the production and distribution of vast quantities of rice to the imperial centers of the north. The wealth that resulted supported, in turn, a money economy, a merchant class engaged in extensive private trading, and the growth of China's provincial cities.

During the Mongol Ascendancy (1264—1368), a flourishing sea trade developed between China, India, and the coast of Southeast Asia. Foreign merchants such as Marco Polo were given special privileges and high office. The Ming Dynasty undertook between 1405 and 1423 a series of great maritime expeditions that eclipsed in scale the European exploits of a century later. Abruptly, in 1424, the Emperor suspended these enterprises, however, and forbade even the construction of seagoing vessels. Students should examine how the Chinese ideal of a unified state under one leader, with a strong bureaucracy controlling the machinery of government, restrained progress. Unable to control the growth of its maritime commerce, the bureaucracy chose instead to withdraw from it.

Students should analyze how Confucian thought supported these actions and returned China to its traditional values. The merchant class was subordinated as a necessary evil of society, and little priority was placed on Chinese trade and manufacturing, which, in A.D. 1000, had been the most advanced in the world. The Chinese invention of printing fostered scholarly study and spread traditional ideas more widely throughout society. The outlook of the Chinese scholarly class came to dominate Chinese thought and government well into the twentieth century. Students should critically analyze the different ways in which Chinese inventions—gunpowder, the compass, and printing—affected China and the West.

Japan

Students will focus next on Japan during the reign of Prince Shotoku (A.D. 592—632). Students should observe Japan's close geographic proximity to the more ancient civilization of China and analyze how that led to the borrowing of ideas, institutions, and technology. At the same time they should consider how its insular location facilitated Japan's political independence, allowing it to borrow selectively and to fashion a culture uniquely its own.

With the establishment of direct relations between the Chinese and Japanese courts in A.D. 607, Japanese artists, craftspersons, scribes, interpreters, and diplomatic dignitaries made frequent visits to China. Members of Japan's upper classes studied Chinese language, literature, philosophy, art, science, and government. Buddhism was introduced and blended with Japan's traditional Shinto religion, "the way of the gods."

Students might compare Chinese poetry and painting appreciated in Japanese imperial courts and urban centers with the distinctive Japanese style of painting that developed in the ninth century and with Noh drama, a unique Japanese art form. By the ninth century Japanese literature was entering its golden age and included the works of several gifted women authors, among them Murasaki Shikibu, whose *Tale of Genji* ranks among the classics of world literature.

The reign of Prince Shotoku becomes the focus for a study of medieval Japan.

Medieval Societies: Europe and Japan

In this unit students will encounter Europe during the High Middle Ages. This study will focus on the economic and political structure of feudal society; daily life and the role of women in medieval times; the growth of towns, trade, and technology; and the development of universities. Special attention should be paid to Christianity in the Middle Ages because the Church, more powerful than any feudal state, influenced every aspect of medieval life. The story of St. Francis of Assisi should be told, both for his embodiment of the Christian ideal and for the accessibility to students of his gentle beliefs. Attention also should be given to the Crusades, with these European undertakings viewed from both the Christian and Muslim vantage points. What were the Crusades? Why did they begin? What were their results?

Students study the economic and political structure of feudal society, including the growth of towns, trade, and technology.

To understand what was distinctive about European culture during this period, students should compare Western Europe with Japan during the High Middle Ages. They will see that the two cultures had aspects in common: a feudal, lord-vassal system, with military leaders (shogun), great lords (daimyo), and knights (samurai). Both feudal societies emphasized personal loyalty to the lord, military skills, a strict code of honor, self-discipline, and fearlessness in battle. Students will also see striking differences in cultural values, religious beliefs, and social customs, including differences in women's roles. Japanese Haiku poetry and European epic poetry such as *Beowulf* provide an interesting contrast. By seeing that some cultural traditions have survived since the Middle Ages, including the importance that Japanese place on family loyalty and ceremonial rituals, students should better understand the meaning of historical continuity. They also should appreciate the significance of change by seeing how much both cultures have been transformed by forces of modernization while retaining aspects of their cultural heritage.

Western Europe and Japan during the High Middle Ages had commonalities: a feudal system and military leaders.

Another aspect of medieval societies that students should understand was the continuing persecution of the Jewish minority; the massacre of Jews by the Crusaders; and the expulsion of Jews from England in 1290, from France in 1306 and 1394, and from many German cities during the time of the Black Death. Students should learn of the conflicts between Christians and Moslems in Spain, beginning in 1085, and the plight of the Jews caught between the warring faiths. Examination of the Spanish and Portuguese inquisitions, during which people were tortured and burned at the stake, should demonstrate the lengths to which religious authorities went to force conversions and to destroy as heretics those who continued in their Judaic faith. The expulsion of the Jews and Moslems from Spain in 1492 should be noted.

Students should note the violations of human rights during the Middle Ages.

Europe During the Renaissance, the Reformation, and the Scientific Revolution

This unit focuses on an unusually rich and important period whose effects continue to influence politics, religion, culture, and the arts of the present day.

A remarkable burst of creativity that began in the fourteenth century in northern Italy and spread through Europe produced the artistic and literary advances of the Renaissance. Classical literature was rediscovered, and humanistic studies flourished. Particular attention should be paid to Florence, Italy, as a major center of commerce, creativity, and artistic genius. Students should be introduced to the writings of Shakespeare, Cervantes, and Machiavelli and to the art of Michelangelo, da Vinci, Botticelli, Raphael, Titian, Van Eyck, and Dürer. Examination of masterpieces such as Michelangelo's *Moses* and Dürer's *The Four Horsemen of the Apocalypse* will demonstrate the powerful vision of these artists as well as the power of art to communicate ideas. Students should analyze how Renaissance painting differed from that of the Middle Ages, even though both reflected many of the same religious themes and symbolisms. They should observe how Renaissance art reflected the advances of that age in science, mathematics, engineering techniques, and understanding of human anatomy.

This unit focuses on an unusually rich and important period whose effects continue to influence politics, religion, culture, and the arts of the present day.

Students should closely examine the Protestant Reformation and become familiar with the religious beliefs of Martin Luther and John Calvin as well as the history of the English Bible. To understand why Luther's 95 theses, nailed to the Wittenberg church door, had such historic results, students should consider the growing religious, political, and economic resistance to the supremacy of the Renaissance popes. Through vivid narrative, attention should be given to the dramatic series of events leading to Luther's excommunication, the peasants' revolt, the spread of the Reformation throughout northern Europe and England, the Catholic response in the Counter-Reformation, the revival of the Inquisition, and the bloody religious conflicts that followed. Most of Germanic Europe became Protestant, while most of Latin Europe remained loyal to Rome. Throughout Europe, the secular power of kings and local rulers grew at the expense of church authority and led to the age of kings. Students should learn the meaning of the divine right of kings, particularly in relation to the French monarchy.

Students should closely examine the Protestant Reformation and its historic results.

The beginnings of modern science can be found in these same tumultuous years of the sixteenth and early seventeenth centuries. Students should draw on their science courses to examine the significance of the methods of scientific observation, mathematical proof, and experimental science developed by such giants of this age as Galileo, Johannes Kepler, Francis Bacon, and Sir Isaac Newton. Students should consider the significance of the inventions of this age—the telescope, microscope, thermometer, barometer, and printing press—and observe how all these developments spurred European leadership in commerce and helped to usher in the age of exploration and the Enlightenment.

The beginnings of modern science can be found in these same tumultuous years of the sixteenth and early seventeenth centuries.

Early Modern Europe: The Age of Exploration to the Enlightenment

This unit begins with the age of exploration, with special attention given to Spanish and Portuguese explorations in the New World. Mapping activities will clarify the routes and empires established in these voyages of exploration and conquest. A brief review of the great heights attained by the Aztec and Incan civilizations should help students place in perspective the plunder and destruction of native cultures that followed the Spanish conquest of these lands. The drama of the Spanish galleons and maritime rivalries between Spain and England culminated in the English defeat of the Spanish Armada in 1588; the consequences of that event should be analyzed.

Northern European seaports thrived as enterprising merchants expanded international commerce. In the 1600s Holland and England welcomed the return of the Jews, who brought their highly developed culture and commercial experience. By focusing on the origins of modern capitalism and the development of a market economy in seventeenth-century Europe, students should deepen their understanding of economics.

This unit concludes with a study of the Enlightenment and its impact on the future of Western political thought, including the political ideas and institutions of the United States. The Enlightenment provoked a clash of ideas between reason and authority, between the natural rights of human beings and the divine right of kings, and between experimentalism in science and dogmatic belief. Students will learn about the major figures of the Enlightenment and their influence on the ways Europeans viewed government and society. They also will see how the principles implicit in the Magna Carta were embodied in the English Bill of Rights, the French Declaration of the Rights of Man and of the Citizen, and the American Declaration of Independence.

Linking Past to Present

This study will conclude with an examination of the political forces let loose in the Western world by the rise of capitalism and the Enlightenment and the impact of the ideas of this period on Western society in the future, especially on the young American republic that the students will be studying in grade eight. To carry this theme into modern times, students will consider the ways in which these ideas continue to influence our nation and the world today; for example, the importance of rationalism in science and technology; the effort to solve problems rationally in local, state, national, and international arenas; and the ideal of human rights, a vital issue today throughout the world.

■ Grade Eight—
United States History and Geography: Growth and Conflict

The eighth-grade course of study begins with an intensive review of the major ideas, issues, and events preceding the founding of the nation. Students will concentrate on the critical events of the period—from the framing of the Constitution to World War I.

Connecting with Past Learnings: Our Colonial Heritage

This year's study of American history begins with a selective review of significant developments of the colonial era with emphasis on the development of democratic institutions founded in Judeo-Christian religious thinking and in English parliamentary traditions; the development of an economy based on agriculture, commerce, and handicraft manufacturing; and the emergence of major regional differences in the colonies.

Connecting with Past Learnings: A New Nation

This unit begins with an in-depth examination of the major events and ideas leading to the American War for Independence. Readings from the Declaration of Independence should be used to discuss these questions: What are "natural rights" and "natural law"? What did Jefferson mean when he wrote that "all men are created equal" and "endowed by their Creator with certain unalienable rights"? What were the "Laws of Nature" and "Nature's God" to which Jefferson appealed?

Close attention should be paid to the moral and political ideas of the Great Awakening and its effect on the development of revolutionary fervor. By reading excerpts from original documents such as sermons of the Great Awakening and Thomas Paine's *Common Sense,* students should be able to understand the revolutionary and moral thinking of the times. Students should become familiar with the debates between Whigs and Tories, the major turning points in the War for Independence, and the contributions of George Washington, Thomas Jefferson, Benjamin Franklin, and other leaders of the new nation. Students should understand the significance that the American Revolution had for other nations, especially France.

The Constitution of the United States

In this unit students concentrate on the shaping of the Constitution and the nature of the government that it created. Students should review the major ideas of the Enlightenment and the origins of self-government in the Magna Carta, the English Bill of Rights of 1689, the Mayflower Compact, the Virginia House of Burgesses, and the New England town meeting. This background will help students appreciate the framers' efforts to create a government that was neither too strong (because it might turn into despotism) nor too weak (as the Articles of Confederation proved to be).

Excerpts from the document written at the Constitutional Convention in Philadelphia should be read, discussed, and analyzed. Students should consider the issues that divided the Founding Fathers and examine the compromises they adopted. Although the Constitution never explicitly mentions slavery, several compromises preserved the institution; namely, the three-fifths rule of representation, the slave importa-

Students concentrate on the critical events of the period—from the framing of the Constitution to World War I.

Students concentrate on the shaping of the Constitution and the nature of the government that it created.

tion clause, and the fugitive slave clause. Why were these provisions so important to southern delegates? Why were these contradictions with the nation's ideals adopted? What were their long-term costs to black men and women and to the nation? To analyze these issues, students must recognize that the American Revolution had transformed slavery from a national to a sectional institution and that nine out of ten American slaves lived in the South. Students should discuss the status of women as reflected in the Constitution of 1787. They should recognize as well the great achievements of the Constitution: (1) it created a democratic form of government based on the consent of the governed—a rarity in history; and (2) it established a government that has survived more than 200 years by a delicate balancing of power and interests and by providing a process of amendment to adapt the Constitution to the needs of a changing society.

Launching the Ship of State

In this unit students consider the enormous tasks that faced the new nation and its leaders through this difficult period; for example, Washington, Jefferson, Madison, Hamilton, and the Adamses. The new nation had to demonstrate that its government would work, and in 1812 it had to fight a war to prove its sovereignty. Students should discuss the belief of the nation's founders that the survival of a democratic society depends on an educated people. Students should analyze the connection between education and democracy symbolized in the Northwest Ordinance and in Jefferson's dictum, "If a nation expects to be ignorant and free, in a state of civilization, it expects what never was and never will be." Attention should be paid to the types of education received in church schools, dame schools, and at home.

Students will become aware of the important connection between education and democracy.

Students also should examine the daily life of ordinary people in the new nation, including farmers, merchants, and traders; women; blacks, both slave and free; and American Indians. Reading excerpts from works by James Fenimore Cooper and Washington Irving will help bring this period alive.

The Divergent Paths of the American People: 1800—1850

This unit follows the nation's regional development in the West, Northeast, and South. Throughout this study students should be encouraged to view historical events empathetically as though they were there, working in places such as mines, cotton fields, and mills.

Students will study the nation's regional development in the West, Northeast, and South and will be encouraged to view historical events empathetically.

The West. The West should be studied for its deep influence on the politics, economy, mores, and culture of the nation. It opened domestic markets for seaboard merchants; it offered new frontiers for discontented Easterners; and it provided a folklore of individualism and rugged frontier life that has become a significant aspect of our national self-image.

The election of Andrew Jackson in 1828 reflected the steady expansion of male suffrage, symbolized the shift of political power to the West, and opened a new era of political democracy in the United States. President Jackson was both a remarkable man and a symbol of his age.

Jacksonian Democracy should be analyzed in terms of the continuing expansion of opportunities for the common person—a recurring theme in American history. The democratizing effect of frontier life on the relations between men and women should be noted. Original documents will show the varied roles played by frontier women such as California's Annie Bidwell, who promoted women's rights and worked for social change.

In studying Jackson's Presidency, students should debate his spoils system, veto of the National Bank, policy of Indian removal, and opposition to the Supreme Court. Alexis de Tocqueville's nine-month visit to the United States at this time, seeking to identify the general principles of democracy in America, can provide students an opportunity to compare his description of national character in the 1830s with American life today.

The story of the acquisition, exploration, and settlement of the trans-Mississippi West, from the Louisiana Purchase in 1803 to the admission of California as a state in 1850, should be reviewed. This was a period marked by a strong spirit of nationalism and "manifest destiny." To deepen their understanding of the changing geography and settlement of this immense land, students might read from the journals of the Lewis and Clark Expedition to the Northwest; map the explorations of trailblazers such as Zebulon Pike; discuss the searing accounts of the removal of Indians and the Cherokees' "Trail of Tears"; and interpret maps and documents relating to the long sea voyages and overland treks that opened the West. Attention should be given to the role of the great rivers and the struggles over water rights in the development of the West. Students should study the northward movement of settlers from Mexico into the great Southwest, with emphasis on the locations of Mexican settlements, their cultural traditions, their attitudes toward slavery, their land-grant system, and the economy they established in these regions. Students need this background before they can analyze the events that followed the arrival of westward-moving settlers from the East into these Mexican territories. Special attention should be given to the Mexican-American War, its territorial settlements, and its aftermath in the lives of the Mexican families who first lived in the region.

Through the story of acquisition, exploration, and settlement, understanding of geography is deepened.

The Northeast. The industrial revolution in the Northeast had important repercussions throughout the nation. Inventions between 1790 and 1850 transformed manufacturing, transportation, mining, communications, and agriculture and profoundly affected how people lived and worked. Skilled craftspersons were replaced by mechanized production in shops, mills, and factories, so well depicted by Charles Dickens in his *American Notes* and in the letters written by young women who left home to work in the mills of Lowell, Massachusetts. Immigrants flocked to the cities. Periods of boom and bust created both progress and poverty.

The industrial revolution transformed manufacturing, mining, communication, agriculture, and education.

An age of reform began that made life more bearable for the less fortunate and expanded opportunities for many. Students should imagine what life was like for young people in the 1830s in order to appreciate Horace Mann's crusade for free public education for all. Students should read excerpts from original documents explaining the social and civic purposes of public education. Typical schoolbooks of the period should be used with attention to their elocution exercises, moral lessons, and orations (for example, *The Columbian Orator*). Role playing should enable students to imagine life in a mill or factory and a day in a Lancastrian school. Students should learn about the major impetus given to the women's rights movement by leaders such as Susan B. Anthony and Elizabeth Cady Stanton. They should read and discuss the Seneca Falls Declaration of Sentiment and compare it with the Declaration of Independence. Efforts by educators such as Emma Willard and Mary Lyon to establish schools and colleges for women should be noted. Major campaigns to reform mental institutions and prisons should be explained by vividly portraying the conditions that evoked them. Students also should become familiar with the work of Dorothea Dix and the significance of Charles Finney as the leader of the second Great Awakening, inspiring religious zeal, moral commitment, and support for the abolitionist movement. Students should examine the relationship of these events to contemporary issues.

The South. During these years, the South diverged dramatically from the Northeast and the West. Its aristocratic tradition and plantation economy depended on a system of slave labor to harvest such cash crops as cotton, rice, sugarcane, and tobacco. Black slavery, the "peculiar institution" of the South, had marked effects on the region's political, social, economic, and cultural development. Increasingly at odds with the rest of the nation, the South was unable to share in the egalitarian surge of the Jacksonian era or in the reform campaigns of the 1840s. Its system of public education lagged far behind the rest of the nation.

The institution of slavery in the South should be studied in its historical context. Students should review their seventh-grade studies of West African civilizations before the coming of the Europeans and compare the American system of chattel slavery, which considered people as property, with slavery in other societies. Attention should be paid to the daily lives of slaves on the plantations, the inhuman practices of slave auctions, the illiteracy enforced on slaves by law, and the many laws that suppressed the efforts of slaves to win their freedom. Students should observe how these laws became increasingly severe following the 1831 slave revolts in South Carolina and Virginia. Particular attention should be paid to the more than 100,000 free blacks in the South and the laws that curbed their freedom and economic opportunity.

The dramatic story of the abolitionist movement, led by people such as Theodore Weld and William Lloyd Garrison, should be told. Attention should be given to what blacks did themselves in working for their own freedom: their organizations, which mobilized legal action; their petitions to Congress for redress of the fugitive slave laws and for emancipation of the slaves; the activities of leading black abolitionists such as Frederick Douglass, Charles Remond, and Sojourner Truth; and the direct actions of free blacks such as Harriet Tubman and Robert Purvis in the underground movement to assist slaves to escape.

The South diverged dramatically from the Northeast and the West in its development.

Excerpts from Frederick Douglass's *What the Black Man Wants,* David Walker's *Appeal,* Harriet Beecher Stowe's *Uncle Tom's Cabin,* and Fanny Kemble's *Description of Life on a Southern Plantation,* as well as excerpts from slave narratives and abolitionist tracts of this period, will bring these people and events alive for students.

Toward a More Perfect Union: 1850—1879

In this unit students concentrate on the causes and consequences of the Civil War. They should discover how the issue of slavery eventually became too divisive to ignore or tolerate. They should understand the significance of such events as the Wilmot Proviso, the Compromise of 1850, the Kansas-Nebraska Act, the Ostend Manifesto, the Dred Scott case, and the Lincoln-Douglas debates. Students should understand the basic challenge to the Constitution and the Union posed by the secession of the southern states and the doctrine of nullification. The war itself should be studied closely, both the critical battlefield campaigns and the human meaning of the war in the lives of soldiers, free blacks, slaves, women, and others. Special attention should be paid to Abraham Lincoln's Presidency, including his Gettysburg Address, the Emancipation Proclamation, and his inaugural addresses.

The Civil War should be treated as a watershed in American history. It resolved a challenge to the very existence of the nation, demolished (and mythologized) the antebellum way of life in the South, and created the prototype of modern warfare. To understand the ordeal of Reconstruction, students should consider the economic ruin, disease, and social chaos that swept the South in the aftermath of the war. They should learn of the postwar struggle for control of the South and of the impeachment of President Andrew Johnson. A federal civil rights bill granting full equality to black Americans was followed by adoption of the thirteenth, fourteenth, and fifteenth amendments. Black citizens, newly organized as Republicans, influenced the direction of southern politics and elected 22 members of Congress. Students should examine the Reconstruction governments in the South; observe the reaction of Southerners toward northern "carpetbaggers" and to the Freedman's Bureau, which sent northern teachers to educate the ex-slaves; and consider the consequences of the 1872 Amnesty Act and the fateful election of 1876, followed by the prompt withdrawal of federal troops from the South.

Students should analyze how events during and after Reconstruction raised and then dashed the hopes of black Americans for full equality. They should understand how the thirteenth, fourteenth, and fifteenth amendments to the Constitution were undermined by the courts and political interests. They should learn how slavery was replaced by black peonage, segregation, Jim Crow laws, and other legal restrictions on the rights of blacks, capped by the Supreme Court's *Plessy* v. *Ferguson* decision in 1896 ("separate but equal"). Racism prevailed, enforced by lynch mobs, the Ku Klux Klan, and popular sentiment. Students also should understand the connection between these amendments and the civil rights movement of the 1960s. Although undermined by the courts

The Civil War should be treated as a watershed in American history.

Events during and after Reconstruction raised and then dashed the hopes of black Americans for full equality. Students study these events in relation to the civil rights movement of the 1960s.

a century ago, these amendments became the basis for all civil rights progress in the twentieth century.

The Rise of Industrial America: 1877—1914

The period from the end of Reconstruction to World War I transformed the nation.

The period from the end of Reconstruction to World War I transformed the nation. This complex period was marked by the settling of the trans-Mississippi West, the expansion and concentration of basic industries, the establishment of national transportation networks, a human tidal wave of immigration from southern and eastern Europe, growth in the number and size of cities, accumulation of great fortunes by a small number of entrepreneurs, the rise of organized labor, and increased American involvement in foreign affairs. The building of the transcontinental railroad, the destruction of the buffalo, the Indian wars, and the removal of American Indians to reservations are events to be studied and analyzed. Reading Chief Joseph's words of surrender to U.S. Army troops in 1877 will help students grasp the heroism and human tragedy that accompanied the conquest of this last frontier. By 1914 the frontier was closed, and the forty-eighth state had entered the Union.

Progress was spurred by new technology in farming, manufacturing, engineering, and producing of consumer goods. Mass production, the department store, suspension bridges, the telegraph, the discovery of electricity, high-rise buildings, and the streetcar seemed to confirm the idea of unending progress, only occasionally slowed by temporary periods of financial distress. Yet, beneath the surface of the "Gilded Age," there was a dark side, seen in the activities of corrupt political bosses; in the ruthless practices of businesses; in the depths of poverty and unemployment experienced in the teeming cities; in the grinding labor of women and children in sweatshops, mills, and factories; in the prejudice displayed against blacks, Hispanics, Catholics, Jews, Asians, and other newcomers; and in the violence associated with labor unrest.

Attention should be given to the developing West and Southwest during these years. The great mines and large-scale commercial farming of this region provided essential resources for the industrial development of the nation. Families from Mexico increasingly provided the labor force that developed this region. Students should understand the social, economic, and political handicaps encountered by these immigrants. Yet, Mexican-American communities survived and even thrived, strengthened by their rich cultural traditions and community life.

Students study the rise of the labor movement and understand the changing role of the government in ameliorating social and economic conditions.

Students should examine the importance of Social Darwinism as a justification for child labor, unregulated working conditions, and laissez-faire policies toward big business. They should consider the political programs and activities of Populists, Progressives, settlement house workers, muckrakers, and other reformers. They should follow the rise of the labor movement and understand the changing role of government in ameliorating social and economic conditions.

The consolidation of public education in the United States and the dramatic growth of public high school enrollments should be noted. By discussing what a typical day was like for their counterparts during these years and reading stories and poems from the *McGuffey Readers,* which were used by more than half the school-age population in the late nineteenth century, students gain a sense of what these schools were like.

This period also was notable for the extension of the United States beyond its borders. Students can trace the major trends in our foreign policy, from George Washington's Farewell Address to the Monroe Doctrine, from our involvement in the Spanish-American War to interventionist policies of Theodore Roosevelt and Woodrow Wilson, culminating in our entry into World War I. By discussing and debating the issues, students should be able to formulate appropriate questions about the American role in these wars.

This period also was notable for the extension of the United States beyond its borders.

Literature should deepen students' understanding of the life of this period, including the immigrant experience, portrayed in Willa Cather's *My Antonia* and O. E. Rolvaag's *Giants in the Earth;* life in the slums, portrayed in Jacob Riis's books; and Mark Twain's *Huckleberry Finn,* unsurpassed as a sardonic commentary on the times.

Linking Past to Present

In this last unit students should examine the transformation of social conditions in the United States from 1914 to the present. They should assess major changes in the social and economic status of blacks, immigrants, women, religious minorities, children, and workers. Students should analyze the economic handicaps on the life chances of a person without an education then and now. They should understand how economic changes have eliminated certain kinds of jobs and created others. They should have a sense of the economic growth in twentieth century America that has drawn most people into the middle class while leaving a significant minority behind.

Students should examine the transformation of social conditions in the United States from 1914 to the present.

To understand the changes that have occurred in social conditions over time, students should analyze the role of the Constitution as a mechanism to guarantee the rights of individuals and to ban discrimination. Teachers should encourage discussion of the citizen's ethical obligation to oppose discrimination against individuals and groups and the converse obligation to work toward a society in which all people enjoy equal rights and a good life. In this unit students should ask themselves: How have things changed over time? Why did these changes occur? They should discuss how citizens in a democracy can influence events and, through participation, apply ethical standards to public life.

The Secondary Curriculum, Grades Nine Through Twelve

Developmental Considerations

The years of early adolescence have been termed a watershed in the development of students' political and historical thought.[1] Students who

---

[1]Joseph Adelson, "The Political Imagination of the Young Adolescent," *Daedalus,* Vol. 100 (fall, 1971), 1013—50.

at age twelve are unable to entertain abstract historical or political ideas or reasoning processes will normally, by age sixteen, have the capacity to engage in analytical thought that is "recognizably adult." This change does not emerge full-blown nor, once under development, is it consistently displayed. High school teachers, just as those in junior high schools, must recognize the continuing need of many students for concrete illustrations and instructional approaches if they are to understand and relate to these political and historical studies. However, the secondary school curriculum must provide learning opportunities that challenge students' growing abstract analytical thinking capabilities if high school students are to be helped to develop these skills.

These more abstract reasoning skills emerge with the adolescent's development of formal thought. Formal thought allows students to develop abstract understanding of historical causality—the often complex patterns of relationships between historical events, their multiple antecedents, and their consequences considered over time. Formal thought also allows students to grasp the workings of political and social systems *as systems* and to engage in higher levels of policy analysis and decision making. In addition, formal thought permits students to deepen and extend their understanding of the more demanding civic learnings: understanding, for example, political conflict in a free society and its resolution under law; understanding the fundamental substantive and procedural values guaranteed by the Constitution; and understanding the close and reciprocating relationships between society and the law within a nation whose Constitution is a charter of principles, not a Napoleonic code.

In this curriculum these advanced historical, political, and civic learnings and advanced critical thinking skills are developed in grades nine through twelve. The course titles for grades nine through twelve with major subtitles are as follows:

Grade Nine—Elective Courses in History-Social Science

- Our State in the Twentieth Century
- Physical Geography
- World Regional Geography
- The Humanities
- Comparative World Religions
- Area Studies: Cultures
- Anthropology
- Psychology
- Sociology
- Women in Our History
- Ethnic Studies
- Law-Related Education

Grade Ten—World History, Culture, and Geography: The Modern World

- Unresolved Problems of the Modern World
- Connecting with Past Learnings: The Rise of Democratic Ideas
- The Industrial Revolution

- The Rise of Imperialism and Colonialism: A Case Study of India
- World War I and Its Consequences
- Totalitarianism in the Modern World: Nazi Germany and Stalinist Russia
- World War II: Its Causes and Consequences
- Nationalism in the Contemporary World
    The Soviet Union and China
    The Middle East: Israel and Syria
    Sub-Saharan Africa: Ghana and South Africa
    Latin America: Mexico and Brazil

Grade Eleven—United States History and Geography: Continuity and Change in the Twentieth Century

- Connecting with Past Learnings: The Nation's Beginnings
- Connecting with Past Learnings: The United States to 1900
- The Progressive Era
- The Jazz Age
- The Great Depression
- World War II
- The Cold War
- Hemispheric Relationships in the Postwar Era
- The Civil Rights Movement in the Postwar Era
- American Society in the Postwar Era
- The United States in Recent Times

Grade Twelve—Principles of American Democracy (One Semester)

- The Constitution and the Bill of Rights
- The Courts and the Governmental Process
- Our Government Today: The Legislative and Executive Branches
- Federalism: State and Local Government
- Comparative Governments, with Emphasis on Communism in the World Today
- Contemporary Issues in the World Today

Grade Twelve—Economics (One Semester)

- Fundamental Economic Concepts
- Comparative Economic Systems
- Microeconomics
- Macroeconomics
- International Economic Concepts

■ Grade Nine—
Elective Courses in History–Social Science

The ninth-grade history–social science curriculum consists of two semesters of elective courses. These courses might consist of two separate topics of one semester each or a two-semester study of a single topic. These courses should build on the knowledge and experience that students have gained in kindergarten through grade eight. They also should contribute substantially to students' preparation for the three *subsequent* years of history–social science education that are mandated in *Education Code* Section 51225.3.

Courses offered should be planned carefully by the district and school and should be consistent with the curricular goals presented in this framework. Placement of students in elective courses should reflect thoughtful counseling at the local school level and should consider the particular needs or interests of the student and the length of time the student has been in the United States. Courses that are not considered appropriate as a history–social science elective include freshman orientation studies, computer literacy, driver training, student government or leadership, drug abuse, career planning, family life education, and courses that reflect state requirements. Such offerings are more appropriate for other departments. The following courses meet the intent and philosophy of this framework:

Our State in the Twentieth Century

This course, which can be presented in one or two semesters, provides students with the opportunity to study contemporary California, its history and geography, its multicultural heritage, its government and economy, the major issues facing the state, and the ways in which students can become active participants in its future.

Opportunities should be included for students to become familiar with the local community through field studies, special community projects, interviews, and other participation activities. In addition, teachers are encouraged to use the community as a major resource for speakers. In drawing on evidence from the present as well as the past, students should learn that individual citizens can influence public policy through participation and can make a difference in the economic, political, and social development of their state.

In studying California's government, students should learn the organization and function of local, county, and state political systems and their relation to the federal government. The role of public education should be included. Study of the legal system should include the procedures of our court system and the basic legal issues relevant to criminal, civil, and juvenile justice. The role and activities of law enforcement should be examined within this context.

Case studies provide students with opportunities to apply and refine critical thinking skills associated with problem solving and civic participation. These studies should focus on contemporary California issues and controversies in such fields as:

- The conflict between increased economic growth and environmental priorities
- The increasing diversity within every aspect of the state: economic, social, cultural, and political
- The types of job opportunities available and the education needed to be employed successfully

By studying contemporary issues, students learn that various forces have brought California to its present position of influence in the United States, the Pacific Basin, and the rest of the world.

Physical Geography

This one-semester course develops the basic themes of physical geography, including a systematic discussion of the physical landscape through geomorphology and topography; the patterns and processes of climate and weather; and water resources through hydrology. These studies equip students with an understanding of the constraints and possibilities that the physical environment places on human development. In addition to these systematic themes, attention is given to the nature of natural resources and their relation to physical geography. Finally, a component of the course is given to place-name geography so that students develop a good sense of where major physical features of the earth are located.

Opportunities for systematic discussion of physical and regional geography are provided.

World Regional Geography

One of the realities of the contemporary world is the increasing influence of other nations in the daily life of the American citizen. This course in World Regional Geography is designed to provide understanding of the distribution and characteristics of the world's major cultures and of the dynamics of human migration and cultural diffusion.

A unit on "The Earth and Its Peoples" introduces basic physical geography and map reading skills. In the remainder of the course, students consider the regional mosaic of the world through a series of studies moving from Western Europe to the Soviet Union and Eastern Europe, the Middle East, and North Africa. They then study sub-Saharan Africa, Asia, the Pacific Basin, and Latin America. For each of these regions, selected nations are studied in depth.

The final unit focuses on Canada and the United States, with emphasis on cultural and political comparisons between these nations and on their economic relationships today. Attention is given to the traditional and contemporary roles foreign nations play in the growth of American culture.

The Humanities

This course focuses on the question, What does it mean to be human? Its purpose is to stretch students' imagination, enrich their experience, and increase their distinctively human potential.[2]

Traditionally, humanities studies have emphasized written works, enriched by the arts of painting, sculpture, architecture, music, drama, and dance. In studying the humanities today, students look not only at books and works of art, but also at buildings, rituals, social groups, and political institutions as examples of the creative power of the human mind and spirit. Recently expanded fields of study have included linguistics, archaeology, architecture, law, the history of religions, and the humanistic approach to science and technology.

---

[2]*Humanities in American Life.* Berkeley: University of California Press, 1980, p. 29.

In designing a humanities course, teachers should draw on the specific records and artifacts of particular people; the things they make, say, or sing; and the expressive forms and objects they create. Classical texts of Western and non-Western cultures should be used. Selections from the arts should be included because they constitute major forms of expression and offer students modes of learning no other discipline provides. Oral cultural forms, film, television, computer-generated designs, and new technology used in the study of cultural artifacts can be introduced. Students' writing should serve as an expressive response to the works of others as well as a major way of forming one's own ideas. The role of racial and ethnic groups within American society and their contributions to our common civilization can be studied in the quest to determine how we came to be what we are today.

Through these varied approaches to the study of the humanities, the teacher fosters critical analysis and understanding, sympathetic insight, perception of the motivations and intentions of others, the ability to distinguish between different values, and the power of the imagination and all the senses to respond intuitively and creatively to the many possibilities of human expression.

Comparative World Religions

Students consider the principal religions of the world that are active today.

In this course students consider the principal religions of the world that are active today, influencing the lives of millions and impressing their image on the contemporary world. Students deal with basic questions: What does humankind believe and what does it worship? In what ways? With what understandings of the ethical life? And with what influence on contemporary times and cultures? In this course students are introduced to:

- Judaism's basis in ethical monotheism; its historic belief in the covenant between God and the Jewish people; the Torah as the source of Judaism's beliefs, rituals, and laws; and the Torah's ethical injunction, "Do justice, love mercy, and walk humbly with thy God"
- Christianity's continuity with Judaism; its belief that Jesus of Nazareth fulfilled Old Testament expectations of the Messiah; and its faith that in His Crucifixion and Resurrection, Jesus Christ reconciled the world to God so that, through forgiveness of sin, the eternal life of God could now flow into the lives of human beings
- Islam's continuity with Judaism and Christianity in its proclamation of belief in one God; its belief that God's will has been given final expression in the Koran in words revealed to the last and the greatest of the prophets, Mohammed; and its observances or the "Five Pillars of Islam"
- Buddhism's origins in the Buddha or Enlightened One; its path of enlightenment through meditation; its ethical mandate to inflict no suffering; and its acceptance of the transmigration of the soul, of Karma, and of Nirvana, the ultimate state of all being

- Hinduism's belief in monism, the oneness of all gods and all living things in the Divine One, Brahma; in pure and unchanging spirit behind the impermanence of the material world; in the peace found only in union with the eternal spirit of Brahma; and in reincarnation, Karma, and Hindu ethics

Beyond these central beliefs, students also develop understandings of the following:

- The explanations given by different religions for the origin of humankind
- The present-day numbers, influence, and geographic distribution of followers of each faith
- The differences between the original tenets of these religions; their historical development; and the major variations in beliefs, sects, or interpretations presently associated with each

Area Studies: Cultures

A course in area studies focuses on an investigation of one or more cultures within a geographic region of the world today; for example, culture studies of the Middle East, Latin America, or Southeast Asia. This study might also compare characteristics of the culture(s) studied with those of similar and diverse cultures.

In the study of a culture, attention should be given to its geographic setting; the population, including traditional and modern family and social life; the status and roles of women and minority groups; and processes of cultural change and exchange. Topics of study should include the philosophies, religions, ideologies, ethics, and values of the culture; its language; its law and education; its literature; its science, mathematics, and medicine; its technology; and its arts, both performing and applied. Attention should be given to the culture's historical, economic, and political developments, including nation building, across time.

Attention should be given to the culture's historical, economic, and political developments, including nation building, across time.

Cultures selected for emphasis could include one that is introduced in the curriculum for kindergarten through grade twelve and presented here to deepen and expand students' knowledge. Cultures also can be chosen to enrich students' understanding of cultural diversity and to provide balance in the representation of ethnic groups and societies around the world.

Anthropology

In this introduction to anthropology, students learn about human beings and their cultures. The two major divisions of anthropology, physical and cultural, are studied.

In physical anthropology students consider the biological characteristics of human beings, their adaptation to their environment, and development in the context of various forms of animal life. In cultural anthropology students learn about the culture of a specific people, past and present, as well as those components of culture universally found among human societies. These components include technology or tools and the ability to use them: language; institutions or organized long-lasting ways of doing things; and beliefs or belief systems. The course includes a study of the evolution of cultures, the organization of societies, processes of enculturation, and the processes and consequences of cultural change. By studying a variety of cultures, students should increase their understanding of their own culture and appreciation of humankind's universal qualities.

Psychology

In this course students are introduced to psychology, with a focus on the scientific study of human development, learning, motivation, and personality. Students should develop some basic concepts of psychology and a historical perspective on psychology as the study of individual behavior. They should read about the contributions of one or more major scholars in the field; for example, Sigmund Freud, Abraham Maslow, Ivan Pavlov, Carl Rogers, and B. F. Skinner. Students should have opportunities to explore implications for everyday life of a scientific perspective on human behavior, and they should learn about the various careers associated with this field of study.

Sociology

In this course students are introduced to sociological concepts, theories, and procedures. Students should learn how sociologists analyze the basic structures and functions of societies and of groups within societies, discover how these societies became organized, identify the conditions under which they become disorganized, and predict the conditions for their reorganization.

The topics studied include the family as the basic unit of society; the structure of groups; group phenomena; the role of the individual in groups; society and communication; personality and the socialization process; social relations and culture; demography and human ecology; social processes; and social control. Sociologists use the scientific method and social research to understand social behavior. Those interested in solving social problems also use these means of investigation together with the application of group processes. Typical study units for this course would include such social issues as crime, poverty, and the problem of discrimination toward the aged and minorities.

Women in Our History

In this course students study the history of American women and analyze the effects historical events have had on women. This history of American women should demonstrate dramatic change as well as continuity. Important advances for women have been related to such developments as improved access to education, knowledge of effective birth-control methods, improvements in household technology, and opportunities to work outside the home.

The complexities of women's changing roles can be studied by using the following outline:

- Women as immigrants and as settlers, 1600—1900 (social change, status, and role)

Students study the history of American women and analyze the effects historical events have had on women.

- Women in the formation of the nation, 1776—1865 (political status, intellectual leadership, and social conscience)
- Women's work and the response to industrialization, 1865—1900 (capital formation, economic exploitation, specialization, and role modification)
- The awakening women's movement in America, 1900—1940 (political justice, social justice, and role of ethnicity)
- The American feminist revolution, 1940 to the present (economic equality, legal equality, and role modification)
- Creative endeavors, past and present

Ethnic Studies

In this course students focus on an in-depth study of ethnic groups, including their history, culture, contributions, and current status in the United States. They learn about the characteristics of America's ethnic groups and the similarities and differences of these groups in both their past and present experiences.

Students focus on an in-depth study of ethnic groups, including their history, culture, contributions, and current status in the United States.

Students should understand the national origins of American ethnic groups. They should study the social, economic, and political forces that caused people to come to America. They should gain insights into the barriers that various ethnic groups have had to overcome in the past and present. They should learn about the opportunities these groups encountered and the contributions made by each to American society. Biographies of individual women and men should be read and analyzed. The experiences of ethnic groups should be examined within their historical context to help students recognize how these events were influenced by the social, economic, and political conditions of the time.

As a result of these studies, students should gain a deeper understanding of American society and its diverse ethnic composition and develop acceptance and respect for cultural diversity in our pluralistic society.

Law-Related Education

In this course students should gain a practical understanding of the law and the legal system that have been developed under the United States Constitution and Bill of Rights. They should become aware of current issues and controversies relating to law and the legal system and be encouraged to participate as citizens in the legal system. Students should be given opportunities to consider their attitudes toward the roles that lawyers, law enforcement officers, and others in the legal system play in our society. In addition, students should be exposed to the many vocational opportunities that exist within the legal system.

Students gain a practical understanding of the law and the legal system that have been developed under the United States Constitution and Bill of Rights.

The course includes a study of concepts underlying the law as well as an introduction to the origin and development of our legal system, including civil and criminal law. In a unit on civic rights and responsibilities, students should learn about the rights guaranteed by the first, fourth, fifth, sixth, eighth, and fourteenth amendments. In a unit on education law, students should study the growing role of the courts in influencing school policy and practice. Mock trials and other simulated legal procedures together with the use of resource experts should help students understand this area.

■ Grade Ten—
World History, Culture, and Geography: The Modern World

In this course students examine major turning points in the shaping of the modern world, from the late eighteenth century to the present. The year begins with an introduction to current world issues and then continues with a focus on the expansion of the West and the growing interdependence of people and cultures throughout the world.

Students examine major turning points in the shaping of the modern world, from the late eighteenth century to the present.

Unresolved Problems of the Modern World

This course begins with a study of major problems in the world today. Examples include government-produced famine in parts of Africa; political instability, poverty, and crushing national debt in Latin America; war and terrorism; the global consequences of destruction of natural resources; economic and cultural dislocations caused by technological change; the proliferation of nuclear weapons; and the struggle to defend human rights and democratic freedoms against governments that respect neither. Each problem will be examined to illustrate the relationships between current issues and their historical, geographic, political, economic, and cultural contexts. Wherever possible, students should be made aware of those organizations that work to alleviate severe problems of poverty, disease, famine, and catastrophe. By discussing specific needs and the various means of sending aid, students can develop a positive response to many world problems and can feel their involvement will make a difference. Students should be encouraged to work on behalf of organizations appropriate to their interests and the point of view of their families.

Connecting with Past Learnings: The Rise of Democratic Ideas

Following an introduction to current world problems, this course will move to a review of the rise of democratic ideas. Students need to know the source of the ideas by which we judge ourselves as a political system and a society. Close attention will be paid to the evolution of democratic principles.

Students need to know the source of the ideas by which we judge ourselves as a political system and a society. Close attention is paid to the evolution of democratic principles.

Students should review the moral and ethical principles of Judaism and Christianity that have profoundly influenced Western democratic thought, including belief in the dignity and equality of all; the search for social systems that ensure the freedom to make individual moral choice; and the duty of each to work for morally just communities.

Students should examine the significance of the Greek philosophers' belief in reason and natural law in relation to democratic ideas. Students should read selections from Plato's *Republic,* Aristotle's *Politics,* and books concerning political life in the city-state of Athens. The teacher should review significant democratic developments in England, particularly the Magna Carta, common law, the Parliament, and the English Bill of Rights of 1689.

Students should review the significant ideas of the Enlightenment thinkers, such as Locke and Rousseau, and their effect on democratic revolutions in England, the United States, France, and Latin America. These revolutions were mileposts in the development of political systems committed to a democratic form of government. The philosophy of natural rights and natural law on which the democratic revolutions were based should be fully discussed and analyzed, with particular attention to the language of the American Declaration of Independence.

Finally, the United States Constitution should be assessed as the summation of this evolving tradition of democratic ideals. Students should understand that political ideals such as equality, justice under law, and freedom, which we now take for granted, were achieved at a high price, remain vulnerable in the West, and are still not practiced in many parts of the world. Although democratic ideals first emerged in the West, almost every nation pays them at least rhetorical homage. In the present world even tyrants feel it necessary to clothe their regimes in the language of democratic ideas. The broad contemporary appeal of these ideas can be found by examining the United Nations' Universal Declaration of Human Rights.

The Industrial Revolution

In the next period of concentrated study, students focus on the Industrial Revolution, beginning in eighteenth century England, and the major changes that the mechanization of production wrought in England's economy, politics, society, culture, and physical environment. Students should examine critical responses to the Industrial Revolution, such as the development of labor unions, the emergence of socialist thought, the Romantic impulse in art and literature (for example, the poetry of William Blake and William Wordsworth and the criticism of John Ruskin and William Morris), and the social criticism of Charles Dickens (for example, *Hard Times*). They also should be aware of successful social reforms, such as the abolition of slavery and reform of the "poor laws." It should be noted that the Industrial Revolution occurred somewhat later, though not with precisely the same consequences, in France, Germany, Japan, and Russia.

Students examine critical responses to the Industrial Revolution.

The Rise of Imperialism and Colonialism: A Case Study of India

In this unit students examine the worldwide imperial expansion that was fueled by the industrial nations' demand for natural resources and markets and by their nationalist aspirations. By studying maps, students will become aware of the colonial possessions of such nations as France, Germany, Italy, Japan, the Netherlands, and the United States.

Study of colonialism in India should begin with a review of Indian history preceding British rule as well as a consideration of the factors that opened India to colonial domination. Throughout the historical study of the Raj (British rule), students should view British imperialism

Students should view British imperialism both from the perspective of the peoples of India and of the colonial rulers.

World War I permanently changed the map of Europe and deeply affected the rest of the world . . . economically, politically, and socially.

both from the perspective of the peoples of India and of the colonial rulers. To understand the cultural conflicts between rulers and ruled, students should examine the principal beliefs of Hinduism, including the caste system, that have shaped the traditional agrarian society of India for more than 5,000 years. The imagery of the *Ramayana* both in art and the oral tradition expresses the continuity and unity of traditional Indian life. Attention should be paid to the role of women in traditional Indian society.

Students should discuss the differing beliefs and values of Hindu and Muslim cultures in India and the British contention that their presence prevented religious conflict. The study should conclude with a brief review of the historical aftermath of colonialism in India up to the present time, including the national movement and the important roles of Mohandas K. Gandhi, Jawaharlal Nehru, and Louis Mountbatten in preparing India for self-government.

World War I and Its Consequences

The growth of nationalism, imperialism, and militarism provides the backdrop for consideration of World War I, which permanently changed the map of Europe and deeply affected the rest of the world. Students should understand the political conditions that led to the outbreak of the war in Europe. Caused in large measure by nationalism, the war stimulated even greater nationalist impulses by dissolving old empires, unleashing irredentist movements, and promoting the spirit of self-determination. Within a context of discussing human rights and genocide, students should learn of the Ottoman government's planned mass deportation and systematic annihilation of Armenian citizens in 1915. Students should also examine the reactions of other governments and world opinion during and after this genocide and the effects on the remaining Armenian population.

Through novels, poems, posters, and films, students should gain an understanding of prewar European culture; of the meaning of total war (targeting civilian populations); of malicious wartime propaganda and false reports of German atrocities; of the opposition to the war in the United States; and of the disillusion that followed the war, including the sense of a world lost, despair over the destruction of a generation of young men, and loss of idealism when the world turned out not to be "safe for democracy" after all. In studying the significant consequences of the war, students should understand the importance of Woodrow Wilson's abortive campaign for the League of Nations; the rise of isolationism in the United States; the punitive terms of the peace imposed on Germany; the Russian Revolution and the national revolutions that resulted in the establishment of independent democratic republics such as Estonia, Latvia, Lithuania, Poland, and Ukraine; the Balfour Declaration (significant in the eventual creation of Israel); the cultural changes after the war (for example, the "lost generation" of Ernest Hemingway, Gertrude Stein, F. Scott Fitzgerald, and others); the impact of Freudian psychology; and the changes wrought by new technology, such as the automobile, radio, and telephone.

Totalitarianism in the Modern World: Nazi Germany and Stalinist Russia

The aftermath of World War I planted the seeds for another world conflict a generation later. A comparison of Nazi Germany and Stalinist Russia will illustrate the methods used by a totalitarian state to extinguish political freedom and to amass total control of society and politics in a single party and single leader. Special attention should be devoted to the destruction of human rights by these two dictatorships. The Holocaust and the famine in Ukraine should receive close attention. This unit offers rich opportunities for analyzing relationships among history, political ideology, governmental structure, economics, cultural traditions, and geography and observing the ways that art and literature can reflect and comment on social conditions.

Students focus attention on the methods used by totalitarian states to suppress freedoms and human rights.

The rise of Hitler should be examined in relation to Germany's postwar economic crisis; the collapse of the Weimar Republic; and Hitler's successful appeal to racism and what the historian Fritz Stern called "the politics of cultural despair." German art, music, and literature (for example, George Grosz and Bertolt Brecht) will deepen students' understanding of this era.

Hitler's policy of pursuing racial purity and its transformation into the Final Solution and the Holocaust should receive close attention. To place Hitler's claim to Aryan superiority in perspective, students should examine the highly developed Jewish culture of central Europe that produced an unusual number of artists such as Marc Chagall, Gustav Mahler, Arnold Schoenberg, and Franz Kafka; scientists such as Albert Einstein and Sigmund Freud; and scholars such as Edmund Husserl and Rudolph Lipschitz.

Hitler's policy of pursuing racial purity and its transformation into the Final Solution and the Holocaust should receive close attention.

Study of the Holocaust should focus students' attention on the systematic suppression of rights and freedoms that preceded the Final Solution. The singular horror of the Holocaust consists not just in the number of people killed, but in the Nazis' ruthless utilization of bureaucratic social organization and modern technology to gather, classify, and eradicate their victims. Previous genocides, such as that perpetrated on the Armenians, already had demonstrated the human capacity for mass murder. The Nazis perfected the social organization of human evil and provided an efficient and frightening model for future despots such as Pol Pot in Cambodia. Students should learn about *Krystallnacht;* about the death camps; and about the Nazi persecution of Gypsies, homosexuals, and others who failed to meet the Aryan ideal. They should analyze the failure of Western governments to offer refuge to those fleeing nazism. They should discuss abortive revolts such as that which occurred in the Warsaw Ghetto, and they should discuss the moral courage of Christians such as Dietrich Bonhoeffer and Raoul Wallenberg, who risked their lives to save Jews.

Numerous films and books (for example, *The Diary of Anne Frank* and Elie Wiesel's *Night*) are available to demonstrate the gruesome reality of the Final Solution. The purpose is not to shock but to engage students in thinking about why one of the world's most civilized nations participated in the systematic murder of millions of innocent people, mainly because of their religious identity.

The Stalin era should be set in the historical context of the czarist regimes with their secret police, censorship, and imprisonment of dissidents. Within this context, students should learn of the many abortive efforts at reform and revolution, the massive underdevelopment of the nation, and the Russian Revolution. Students should examine the Bolshevik overthrow of the Kerensky government and understand the difference between the Bolsheviks and the Mensheviks. They should recognize the roles of Lenin, Trotsky, and Stalin; and they should analyze the meaning of communist ideology.

With Stalin's rise to power, students should perceive the connection between economic policies, political policies, the absence of a free press, and systematic violations of human rights. With this background they should examine the forced collectivization of agriculture; the murder of millions of kulaks; the government-created famine in Ukraine that led to the starvation of millions of people; the political purges of party leaders, artists, engineers, and intellectuals; and the show trials of the 1930s.

By analyzing examples of socialist realist art and reading Yevgeny Zamyatin's *We,* the first antiutopian novel, and Arthur Koestler's classic *Darkness at Noon,* students will acquire deeper insights into this period.

Students should understand the danger of concentrating unlimited power in the hands of a central government.

As a result of this in-depth study, students should understand the nature of totalitarian rule and recognize the danger of concentrating unlimited power in the hands of the central government. They should develop understanding of the importance of a free press, the right to criticize the government without fear of reprisal, an independent judiciary, opposition political parties, free trade unions, and other safeguards of individual rights. This is an appropriate point at which to reflect on the role of the individual in mass society. What is the ethical responsibility of the individual when confronted with governmental actions such as the Final Solution and other violations of human rights?

World War II: Its Causes and Consequences

Students analyze the causes and consequences of World War II.

The study of nazism and Stalinism leads directly to an analysis of World War II and its causes and consequences. Students should realize which major nations formed the Allied and the Axis Powers. They should understand the significance of the Nazi-Soviet Nonaggression Pact and its effects in partitioning Poland and bringing Latvia, Lithuania, and Estonia under Soviet control. They should examine the German offensive, the battle of Britain, the major turning points of the war (for example, Stalingrad and the Normandy invasion), and the effects of the Yalta Conference.

Attention should be given to the war in the Pacific, including Japan's prewar expansion in east and southeast Asia, its attack on Pearl Harbor, and the struggle for the Pacific. In discussing President Truman's decision to use the atomic bomb against Japan, students might read John Hersey's *Hiroshima,* contemporary newspaper accounts, and the autobiographical statements of those involved.

Particular attention should be paid to the consequences of World War II, which continue to have so much importance in shaping the contemporary world. Students should discuss the importance of the Marshall Plan and the Truman Doctrine (targeted to Greece and Turkey), which established the pattern for the postwar American policy of supplying economic and military aid to prevent the spread of communism and to assist the economic development of our allies. American assistance to Japan and Germany contributed to their phenomenal postwar reconstruction and their emergence as major world economic powers.

A study of Poland should provide understanding of the consequences of World War II for the nations of Eastern Europe. In addition to the more than three million Polish Jews slaughtered, approximately one-half million other Poles were systematically executed, including Poland's political and military leaders, church leaders who spoke out against nazism, and educators. Then, in agreements reached in the Tehran, Yalta, and Potsdam conferences, Western leaders abandoned the Polish government-in-exile and acquiesced to Stalin's demands for Poland. Mass arrests of noncommunist leaders, expropriation of private land, and nationalization of industry followed. Despite decades of strikes, protests, and the organization of industrial workers in the Solidarity movement, the Soviet-dominated regime retained its power. Students should analyze how a nondemocratic government retains power without the consent of the governed and the institutions it destroys to maintain its control (for example, free elections, competing political parties, freedom of speech and religion, a free press, free trade unions, and an independent judiciary).

Other important postwar developments to be studied include the establishment of the state of Israel; the creation of the United Nations; the Warsaw Pact, SEATO, and NATO; the Cold War; the Korean War; the Hungarian Revolution; and the Vietnam War and its aftermath, particularly the genocide committed in Cambodia by the Pol Pot regime.

Postwar developments are studied.

Nationalism in the Contemporary World

The last major topic in this course is the study of nationalism in the contemporary world, illustrated by brief analyses of four pairs of nations that are connected either by political ideology (Soviet Union and China) or by regional location (Israel and Syria, Ghana and South Africa, and Mexico and Brazil). In the development of these case studies, particular attention should be paid to the connections among political systems, economic development, and individual rights. By analyzing the problems that these studies illustrate, students should be able to understand major national and international dilemmas occurring today.

The study of nationalism in the contemporary world is presented through case studies.

The Soviet Union and China. A comparative study of the Soviet Union and China offers students an instructive comparison of two contemporary societies that have become world powers because of their size, military might, natural resources, and economic potential. Both were created in the twentieth century as a result of communist revolu-

Study of the Soviet Union and China offers a comparison of two contemporary societies that have become world powers.

89

tions. Both were underdeveloped countries whose leaders imposed collectivist means to modernize the economy and the society. In comparing these two nations, students must understand the conditions that preceded the revolution, their revolutionary leaders (Lenin, Stalin, and Mao), the nature of communist ideology, and the human consequences of both revolutions: the millions of "class enemies" and political dissidents who were murdered during and after the revolutions, the stifling of religious freedom, the conformity imposed on artists and intellectuals, the economic disruptions caused by forced collectivization, and the establishment of party elites who exert absolute control over the government and media.

In this unit students have an opportunity to discuss differences among revolutions. What is a revolution? Why are some revolutions, such as the French Revolution and communist revolutions, followed by political purges and mass killings? Why are others, such as the American Revolution, followed by the establishment of democratic institutions and mechanisms for orderly change?

Geopolitical analyses (such as the drive for warm water ports and agricultural resources) should be introduced in considering Soviet hegemony in Eastern Europe (for example, Poland, Hungary, Czechoslovakia, Yugoslavia, and the Baltic States) and Chinese aspirations in Asia. Students should read excerpts from Nikita Khrushchev's speech of 1956 denouncing the crimes of Joseph Stalin, Aleksandr Solzhenitsyn's *The Gulag Archipelago,* and memoirs describing the Chinese Cultural Revolution. Examination of current problems should demonstrate the ways in which today's leaders are attempting to modify their political and economic structures by incorporating elements of a free market economy.

The Middle East: Israel and Syria. Since World War II the Middle East has been a political hotbed unsettled by the passions of nationalism and religion. This region has been in almost continual ferment not only because of wars between Israel and the Arab nations but also because of tensions between Arab nations and among different Islamic groups, including the differences between Sunni and Shiite Muslims. The fragile political affairs of the area are further aggravated by its strategic importance as a supplier of oil to the industrialized world, the unresolved problems of the displaced Palestinian refugees, the recurrent use of terrorism among adversaries, the disruptions associated with the interaction of traditional cultures and the forces of modernization, and the importance of this region as a focus of East-West rivalries. Careful study of political and resource maps should help students understand the relative location and the geopolitical, cultural, military, and economic significance of such key states as Saudi Arabia, Turkey, Syria, Lebanon, Jordan, Israel, Kuwait, Iraq, and Iran. Students can more deeply analyze the problems of this vital region by an examination of two strategically important states, Israel and Syria.

A brief review of the history of Israel should include the importance of the land in Jewish religious history and should trace the history of

Students analyze the problems of the Middle East by examining two strategically important states, Israel and Syria.

Zionism, with special reference to the Holocaust as a factor in the creation of Israel in 1948. Attention should be paid to its democratic parliamentary government, free press, and independent judiciary. Students should understand such problems as the difficulty of accommodating the demands of orthodox religious groups, the internal debate over the West Bank, the conflict between Jews and Arabs within Israel, an economy overburdened by military expenditures, and Israel's precarious existence in a hostile region.

Students should trace Syria's long history and examine its present status as a strategically important Arab nation. Syria should be seen within the context of a region that has sought Pan Arab unity while working to overcome problems of illiteracy, shortage of health services, ethnic rivalries, and religious tensions. Attention should be paid to the form of government in Syria, the status of minorities, government control of the media, and Syria's regional and military importance in the world today.

Sub-Saharan Africa: Ghana and South Africa. In this unit on sub-Saharan Africa in the twentieth century, students should examine the west coast nation of Ghana and the nation of South Africa. Both nations should be studied in their historic and geographic context and in their international relationships within today's increasingly complex and interdependent world.

Ghana and South Africa are studied in their historic and geographic context and in their international relationships in today's world.

As they begin their study of Ghana, students should review briefly the once-great kingdoms of Ghana and Mali, which were studied in grade seven. They should learn that between the seventeenth and nineteenth centuries more than ten million Africans were enslaved and transported to the Western Hemisphere; about 400,000 of these were brought to British North America. Students should recognize that the African slave trade existed centuries before the first European contacts; however, the acute labor shortage in the New World created a vast new market for slave labor and systematically depleted Africa of successive generations of young men and women. This social, cultural, and economic disruption of West Africa was further aggravated in the late nineteenth century by the introduction of European colonization and economic exploitation of the region. Students should analyze the effects of centuries of exploitation on African states that have only recently achieved their independence from colonial rule.

A case study of Ghana today should provide students a graphic example of the political and economic problems of one African nation, a former British colony and the first to gain its independence. This nation, rich in gold resources and once the world's largest cocoa producer, is working to overcome the economic collapse engendered during its 26 years under socialism.

In South Africa the large settlement of Europeans has complicated human and cultural relations, with results culminating in political and racial crises. Students should observe how the government of South Africa developed out of European colonial roots and how its system of apartheid denies legal equality and political participation to the black majority. The political tensions in South Africa should be analyzed for their effects throughout the entire region. Students can engage in activities such as debating the future of South Africa from the perspectives of a leader of the white minority government, a black nationalist leader, and a spokesperson for the white liberals in South Africa. Reading excerpts from Mark Mathabane's autobiography, *Kaffir Boy,* will give students insight into growing up as a black under apartheid.

Latin America: Mexico and Brazil. In this unit students examine two developing Latin American nations, Mexico and Brazil. This unit begins with a geographic overview of Central and South America, including the region's political divisions, natural features, resources, and population patterns. The unit continues with a case study of present-day Mexico, a nation strong in its sense of national identity and proud of its indigenous heritage and its Hispanic past. Confronting Mexico today are problems of undereducation and an economic capacity that is insufficient to employ the nation's burgeoning population. Students should analyze the domestic as well as the international economic and political causes and consequences of these problems. Students should consider Mexico's relationship with its Hispanic neighbors, with whom it exerts considerable national leadership in pressing for Hispanic solutions to hemispheric problems. They should also consider Mexico's relationships with the Yankee colossus to its north, including the lure that the United States holds for Mexico's people seeking economic opportunity.

In the unit on Brazil, students should examine the cultural diversity of the nation, including its immigrant population from many nations; and the economic contrasts between its highly industrialized southern cities, its agricultural and mineral wealth, and its sporadically settled interior regions. Students can compare the burgeoning growth of Brazil's major cities with that of Mexico City and analyze the social, economic, and political problems that are created as the rural poor continue to move to these cities.

Attention should be given to resettlement programs of the vast interior of Brazil, including the Amazon. Students should analyze the massive destruction of the tropical rain forests as settlers speculate in ranching and agriculture; the long-term costs to the earth's biosphere as these irreplaceable forests are systematically destroyed; the countless species of wildlife and vegetation lost; and the future of this region as grasses lose their nutritional value in these regions of shallow soil and speculative ranches are abandoned.

In all of these studies, students should develop understanding of the historic as well as the contemporary geographic, social, political, and economic contexts in which these problems have arisen and which must be taken into account if each nation's contemporary problems and national aspirations are to be understood. It is especially important at this grade level that students be presented with differing perspectives on these issues and events in order to develop the critical thinking skills of an informed citizen in the contemporary world.

Students examine two developing Latin American nations.

It is important that students be presented with differing perspectives on issues and events in order to develop the critical thinking skills of an informed citizen in the contemporary world.

■ Grade Eleven—
United States History and Geography: Continuity and Change in the Twentieth Century

In this course students examine major turning points in American history in the twentieth century. During the year certain themes should be emphasized: the expanding role of the federal government and federal courts; the continuing tension between the individual and the state and between minority rights and majority power; the emergence of a modern corporate economy; the impact of technology on American society and culture; change in the ethnic composition of American society; the movements toward equal rights for racial minorities and women; and the role of the United States as a major world power. In each unit students should examine American culture, including religion, literature, art, drama, architecture, education, and the mass media.

The year begins with a selective review of United States history, with an emphasis on two major themes—*the nation's beginnings,* linked to the tenth-grade retrospective on the Enlightenment and the rise of democratic ideas; and *the industrial transformation of the new nation,* linked to the students' tenth-grade studies of the global spread of industrialism during the nineteenth century.

Students examine major turning points in American history in the twentieth century as they reflect continuity and change from the nation's beginnings.

Connecting with Past Learnings: The Nation's Beginnings

In this first review unit, students should draw on their earlier studies (in grades seven, eight, and ten) of the Enlightenment and the rise of democratic ideas as the context in which this nation was founded. Special attention should be given to the ideological origins of the American Revolution and its grounding in the democratic political tradition, Judeo-Christian ideals, and the natural rights philosophy of the Founding Fathers. Special attention also should be given to the framing of the Constitution as background for understanding the contemporary constitutional issues raised throughout this course.

Special attention is given to the framing of the Constitution as background for understanding the contemporary constitutional issues raised throughout this course.

Connecting with Past Learnings: The United States to 1900

In this second review unit, students should concentrate on the testing of the new nation through the Civil War and the nineteenth century growth of the nation as an industrial power. First, students should review the history of the Constitution after 1787, with particular attention given to the issue of federal versus state authority, a question that was resolved only by the Civil War. The war and the Reconstruction of the federal union that followed should be highlighted.

Second, students should review the growth of the United States as an industrial and world power. A brief retrospective of the grade ten study of the industrial revolution should set the global context for America's industrial development. Other emphases in this review unit should include the significance of immigration in producing ethnic diversity, the demographic shifts of the nineteenth century, and the emergence of the United States in the late nineteenth century as a world power. Again, reference should be made to grade ten studies of nineteenth century European imperialism as the global context in which America's growing influence as a world power was established.

The Progressive Era

In the first in-depth study of the year, students learn about the Progressive Era, a period rich with controversy and change. Students should understand the combination of massive immigration and industrialization that produced vast urban slums with intolerable living and working conditions and crowded, inadequate schools. They should examine the corporate mergers that produced trusts and cartels, industrial giants, "robber barons," and the gaudy excesses of the Gilded Age. They should study examples of the corrupt big-city machines that delivered services to the immigrant poor in exchange for votes. They should discuss the philosophy of Social Darwinism as well as the religious reformism associated with the ideal of the Social Gospel. The work of social reformers such as Jane Addams to improve living conditions for the poor and downtrodden should be noted. Excerpts from the works of muckrakers such as Lincoln Steffens, Jacob Riis, Ida Tarbell, and Joseph Mayer Rice and novels by writers such as Theodore Dreiser, Upton Sinclair, and Frank Norris will help set the scene. These social conditions should be seen as background for the progressive reform movement that challenged big-city bosses; rallied public indignation against "the trusts"; led successful campaigns for social and economic legislation at the city, state, and federal levels; and played a major role in national politics in the pre-World War I era. Students should examine the impact of mining and agriculture on the laws concerning water rights during these years. As a result of progressive legislation, the role of the federal government in regulating business and commerce was expanded during the administrations of Theodore Roosevelt and Woodrow Wilson.

Students should analyze the nation's foreign policy, especially President Theodore Roosevelt's "big stick" policies and the United States' involvement in World War I. They should review their tenth-grade study of the causes and consequences of World War I and its projection of the United States into world affairs. Students should learn about President Woodrow Wilson's Fourteen Points and the League of Nations. They should discuss domestic opposition to the war, prejudice toward German Americans, and the nation's reversion to isolationism.

Popular fears of communism and anarchism associated with the Russian Revolution and World War I provoked attacks on civil liberties; for example, the postwar Palmer Raids, the "Red Scare," the Sacco-Vanzetti case, and legislation restraining individual expression and privacy. Legal challenges to these activities produced major Supreme Court decisions defining the right to dissent and freedom of speech. By reading some of the extraordinary decisions of Justices Louis Brandeis and Oliver Wendell Holmes, students will understand the continuing tension between the rights of the individual and the power of government. Students can consider such questions as: Who speaks for unpopular causes in American society? Is such a voice needed in a society controlled by majority vote? This is an appropriate point to discuss the founding of organizations such as the American Civil Liberties Union (ACLU) and the National Association for the Advancement of Colored People (NAACP) to defend unpopular views and minority rights.

As the Progressive Era ended, women won the right to vote with the passage of a constitutional amendment establishing women's suffrage. What were the arguments for and against female suffrage? How is the Constitution amended?

The Jazz Age

The 1920s had no single event such as a war or a depression around which to organize its story, but the decade was nonetheless colorful and important. It is usually characterized as a period of Prohibition, gangsters, speakeasies, jazz bands, and flappers, living frivolously as the economic disaster of the 1930s inexorably drew near. This in-depth study should be used to test the complex realities of this era. Students should recognize the change from the reformism of the Progressive Era to the desire for "normalcy" in the 1920s as evidenced by the election of Warren Harding, Calvin Coolidge, and Herbert Hoover. What was normalcy to some was reaction to others, however, as Congress restricted immigration on the basis of nationality quotas, Ku Klux Klan activities increased in the South and Midwest, farm income declined precipitously, and labor unrest spread throughout the country.

Students study in depth the decade of the 1920s and test the complex realities of this important era.

For most Americans, however, the standard of living rose, and new consumer goods such as automobiles, radios, and household appliances became available. Students should learn how the widespread adoption of mass production techniques such as the assembly line helped to make American workers highly efficient. The emergence of the mass media created new markets, new tastes, and a new popular culture. Movies, radio, and advertising spread styles, raised expectations, and promoted interest in fads and sports. At the same time, major new writers began to appear, such as William Faulkner, F. Scott Fitzgerald, and Sinclair Lewis.

A migration of many blacks from the South helped to create the "Harlem Renaissance," the literacy and artistic flowering of black artists, poets, musicians, and scholars, such as W.E.B. Du Bois, Langston Hughes, Richard Wright, and Zora Neale Hurston. Examples of their work should be read. Marcus Garvey, the black nationalist leader of a Back to Africa movement, reached the peak of his popularity during this period.

The Great Depression

The Great Depression of the 1930s brought major changes in American politics, society, and culture.

The collapse of the national and international economies in 1929 led to the Great Depression of the 1930s and major changes in American politics, society, and culture. Although the political culture of the 1920s exuded self-confidence and optimism, the Depression caused many people to question the viability of American institutions. One reaction to the economic crisis and the rise of fascism in Europe was the growth of extremist political movements on the right and the left.

Students should assess the likely causes of the Depression and examine its effects on ordinary people in different parts of the nation through use of historical materials. They should recognize the way in which natural drought combined with unwise agricultural practices to cause the Dust Bowl, a major factor in the economic and cultural chaos of the 1930s. They should see the linkage between severe economic distress and social turmoil. Photographs, films, newspaper accounts, interviews with persons who lived in the period, as well as paintings and novels (such as John Steinbeck's *Grapes of Wrath*) will help students understand this critical era.

The administration of Franklin D. Roosevelt and his New Deal should be studied as an example of the government's response to economic crisis. The efforts of the Roosevelt Administration to alleviate the crisis through the creation of social welfare programs, regulatory agencies, and economic planning bureaus should be carefully assessed. President Roosevelt's dominance of American politics should not obscure the significant opposition to his policies. Students should have an accurate sense of the controversy generated by the New Deal and of the attacks on Roosevelt. Students should read excerpts from Roosevelt's memorable inaugural addresses and fireside chats in order to perceive the President's efforts to rally the nation's spiritual energy. Events during Roosevelt's Presidency mark the beginning of what some historians have called the "Imperial Presidency." The crises of the Depression, World War II, and postwar international tensions have caused a dramatic expansion of the power of the presidency. Students should analyze the risk to separation of powers caused by this phenomenon and the continuing danger to representative government that this trend implies.

World War II

World War II had far-reaching effects on both the United States and the world.

In this unit students examine the role of the United States in World War II. Students should review the rise of dictatorships in Germany, the Soviet Union, and Japan; and they should examine the events in Europe and Asia in the 1930s that led to war. Students should understand the debate between isolationists and interventionists in the United States as well as the effect on American public opinion of the Nazi-Soviet pact and the bombing of Pearl Harbor. Students should look again at the Holocaust and consider the response of Franklin D. Roosevelt's Administration to Hitler's atrocities against Jews and other groups.

By reading contemporary accounts in newspapers and popular magazines, students should understand the extent to which this war taught Americans to think in global terms. By studying wartime strategy and major military operations, students should grasp the geopolitical implications of the war and its importance for postwar international relations. The controversy over President Harry S Truman's decision to drop atomic bombs on Japan should be analyzed fully, considering both his rationale and differing historical judgments.

Attention should be paid to the effect of the war on the home front. Industrial demands fueled by war needs contributed to ending the Depression and set a model for an expanded governmental role after the war. Wartime factory work created new job opportunities for unskilled women and blacks. The racial segregation of the armed forces, combined with the egalitarian ideology of the war effort, produced a strong stimulus for civil rights activism when the war ended. The relocation and internment of 110,000 Japanese Americans during the war on grounds of national security was a governmental decision that should be analyzed as a violation of their human rights.

The relocation and internment of 110,000 Japanese Americans during the war on grounds of national security was a governmental decision that should be analyzed as a violation of their human rights.

The Cold War

In this unit students focus on the postwar relations between the United States and the Soviet Union. Students should examine the Soviet conquest of Eastern Europe and its takeover of Poland, Hungary, and Czechoslovakia. As part of their study of President Truman's policy of containment of communism, students should examine the Truman Doctrine, the Marshall Plan, the creation of the North Atlantic Treaty Organization, and the Berlin blockade and airlift. They should be aware of the Soviet Union's violations of human rights during this period. The controversy among historians over the causes of the Cold War should be discussed.

Study of the Cold War focuses on the tensions that remained between the United States and the Soviet Union.

The domestic political response to the spread of international communism should receive attention as part of the study of the Cold War. Students should learn about the investigations of domestic communism at the federal and state levels and about the celebrated spy trials of the period. As part of this unit, students should discuss the censure of Senator Joseph McCarthy by his colleagues in the U.S. Senate. Students should debate the appropriateness of loyalty oaths (an important issue at the University of California in the 1950s) and legislative investigations of people's beliefs. During this era there were significant Supreme Court decisions that protected citizens' rights to dissent and freedom of speech.

The study of the foreign policy consequences of the Cold War should be extended to an examination of the major events of the administrations of Dwight D. Eisenhower, John F. Kennedy, and Lyndon B. Johnson. Students should examine the United Nations' intervention in Korea, Eisenhower's successful conclusion of that conflict, and his administration's defense policies based on nuclear deterrence and massive retaliation. Foreign policy during the Kennedy and Johnson administrations represents a continuation of Cold War strategy, with the emphasis shifting to guerrilla warfare in Southeast Asia and leading to the Vietnam War. These events should be placed within the context of continuing tensions between the Soviet Union and the United States.

President Eisenhower's warning about the rise of a "military-industrial complex," created during World War II and maintained to meet the military threat of Soviet expansionism, raises important issues for students to discuss: What is the role of conventional forces in a nuclear age? How important to the economy of states and localities are defense industries? What effect does research for military purposes have on our economic productivity and competitiveness? What is the appropriate balance between "guns and butter" or between military and civilian needs? How are these questions decided in our political system?

Hemispheric Relationships in the Postwar Era

In this unit students should consider the nation's postwar relationships with Latin America and Canada. Students should examine the events leading to the Cuban Revolution of 1959; the political purges and the economic and social changes enforced by Castro; the introduction of Soviet influence and military aid in the Caribbean; the 1961 Bay of Pigs invasion and the 1962 Missile Crisis; the 1965 crisis in the Dominican Republic; the 1978 Panama Canal Treaty; and the spread of Cuban influence, indigenous revolution, and counterrevolution in Nicaragua and El Salvador in the 1980s. Students should analyze the continuing involvement of the United States in this region.

An analysis of U.S. economic relationships with the nations of Latin America today should include the international as well as domestic causes of mounting third world debt in Latin America and the global interrelatedness of the economies of this hemisphere and the world.

A study of postwar relationships between the United States and Canada should note the long history of peaceful, negotiated settlement of problems between these nations. To understand recent problems, students should become sensitive to the Canadian perspective and to Canada's heavy economic dependence on its forest products and its oceanic fishing grounds. Attention should be given to the issues arising from Canada's government-subsidized trade in forest products and the U.S. response of adopting protective tariffs. In turning to the World Court to settle fishing rights to the prolific Georges Bank fishing grounds off Nova Scotia, the United States and Canada provide an important case study in peaceful arbitration between nations. Among the unresolved problems confronting these two nations is the problem of acid rain, an issue of global interdependence that concerns other nations in the industrialized world today.

The Civil Rights Movement in the Postwar Era

In this unit students should focus on the history of the civil rights movement in the 25 years after World War II and on the dramatic social and political transformations that it brought. The emphasis in this unit is on the application of the Constitution and the Bill of Rights in modern times to the resolution of human rights issues. Students should understand the central role black Americans have played in this century in expanding the reach of the Constitution to include all Americans.

A review of earlier learnings should help students grasp the enormous barriers black Americans had to overcome in their struggle for their rights as citizens. Attention should be given to the provisions enacted into the Constitution in 1787 that preserved slavery; the post-Civil War laws and practices that reduced the newly freed slaves to a state of peonage; and the Jim Crow laws that were upheld by the Supreme Court in a series of decisions in the late nineteenth century. Students should be aware of Booker T. Washington, the founder of Tuskegee Institute. Excerpts from his 1895 Atlanta Exposition address will show his efforts to adjust to the handicaps of racial segregation. Discrimination continued to confront black citizens who migrated to northern cities and who served in world wars I and II.

Readings from Gunnar Myrdal's *An American Dilemma* will help students analyze the contrast between the American creed and the practices of racial segregation throughout the nation in the years preceding World War II. What was the dilemma? What is the creed that Myrdal stressed? As background, students must understand the meaning of "separate but equal," both as a legal term and as a reality that effectively limited the life chances of black Americans by denying them equal opportunity for jobs, housing, education, health, and voting rights.

Students should learn about the rise of the civil rights movement and the legal battle to abolish segregation. The battle in the courts began with challenges to racial segregation in higher education and achieved a signal victory in 1954 with the *Brown* v. *Board of Education of Topeka* decision. This important decision should be read and discussed. Students should analyze why one of the first demands of the civil rights movement was for equal educational opportunity. Why is education so important in the life chances of an individual? What happens to people who are not educated in America today? What kinds of jobs can they get? How does mass illiteracy affect an entire society? (Here students should review what they learned in the tenth-grade unit on "Nationalism in the Contemporary World.") What would life in the United States be like if there were no public schools? Interviews and case studies can be made of successful men and women from minority groups whose lives have changed because of their education.

The *Brown* decision stimulated a generation of political and social activism led by black Americans pursuing their civil rights. Momentous events in this story illumine the process of change: the commitment of white people in the South to "massive resistance" against desegregation; the Montgomery bus boycott, which was started by Rosa Parks and then led by the young Martin Luther King, Jr.; the clash in Little Rock, Arkansas, between federal and state power; the student sit-in demonstrations that began in Greensboro, North Carolina; the "freedom rides"; the march on Washington in 1963; the Mississippi Summer Project of 1964; and the march in Selma, Alabama, in 1965. Students should recognize how these dramatic events influenced public opinion and enlarged the jurisdiction of the federal courts. They should understand Dr. King's philosophical and religious dedication to nonviolence by reading documents such as his "Letter from a Birmingham Jail," and

The legal battle to abolish racial segregation achieved a signal victory in 1954 with the Brown *decision.*

they should recognize the leadership of the black churches in the movement. By viewing films of this period, students should recognize both the extraordinary moral courage of ordinary black men, women, and children and the interracial character of the civil rights movement.

The expansion of the role of the federal government as a guarantor of civil rights should be examined, especially during the administrations of Presidents Kennedy and Johnson. After President Kennedy's assassination, Congress enacted landmark federal programs in civil rights, education, and social welfare. Students should examine the historical significance of the Civil Rights Act of 1964 and the Elementary and Secondary Education Act of 1965.

The peak of legislative activity in 1964-65 was accompanied by a dramatic increase in civil unrest and protest among urban blacks, and 1966 saw the emergence of the Black Power movement. The assassination of Dr. King in 1968 deprived the civil rights movement of its best-known leader, but not its enduring effects on American life. In considering issues such as school busing and group quotas, students can discuss the continuing controversy between group rights to a fair share as opposed to individual rights to equal treatment. Well-chosen readings should heighten students' sensitivity to the issues raised in this unit, such as *The Autobiography of Malcolm X,* Lerone Bennett's *Before the Mayflower: A History of Black America,* Ralph Ellison's *Invisible Man,* Richard Wright's *Native Son,* and Lorraine Hansberry's *A Raisin in the Sun.*

The successful example of the black civil rights movement encouraged other groups—including women, Hispanics, American Indians, and the handicapped—in their campaigns for legislative and judicial recognition of their civil equality. Major events in the development of all these movements and their consequences should be noted.

American Society in the Postwar Era

Students focus on significant social, economic, and political changes following World War II.

In this unit students focus on other significant social, economic, and political changes of the 25 years following World War II. Having emerged from the war with a strong industrial base, the nation experienced rapid economic growth and a steady increase in the standard of living. The GI Bill of Rights opened college doors to millions of returning veterans who contributed to the nation's technological capacity. The economic surge was extended during the Eisenhower era, which was marked by low inflation, social calm, and political quiescence.

Students should examine the significance of the Supreme Court under the leadership of former California Governor Earl Warren. Decisions of this court made sweeping changes in many areas of American life. Beyond the *Brown* decision (already studied), consideration should be given to decisions affecting criminal due process, voting rights, freedom of speech, and other areas of expression that have affected our lives dramatically. Students should be prepared to debate the question of the role of the courts in overturning laws passed by Congress and state legislatures. Historical depth should be provided by comparing the Warren Court to the Hughes Court of the 1930s, both of which used judicial power to invalidate statutes passed by democratically elected legislatures.

Students should read about the beginning of the environmental movement in the 1960s and the environmental protection laws that were passed. The expansion of the war in Vietnam provoked antiwar protests that reflected and contributed to a deep rift within American culture. From within the protest movement, a "counterculture" emerged with its own distinctive style of music, dress, language, and films. When the war ended, the counterculture was absorbed in the mainstream.

The Vietnam War, a major event of the 1960s, continues to have implications 20 years later.

The Nixon Administration (1968—1974) was notable for establishing relations with the People's Republic of China, opening a period of detente with the Soviet Union, and negotiating a withdrawal of American troops from Vietnam. Despite his skill in managing foreign affairs, Richard Nixon's Administration was marred by a political scandal called Watergate that led to his resignation in 1974. Students should understand the events that led to President Nixon's resignation, and they should assess the role of the courts, the press, and the Congress. Students can discuss the continuing issue of unchecked presidential power. Are the President and his staff above the law?

The study of this fascinating period should include an examination of the continuing economic boom that began in 1940-41 and the growth of the middle class, with poverty concentrated among minority groups, the elderly, and single-parent families.

Major attention should be given to demographic changes, such as the Baby Boom, white flight to the newly developing suburbs, the migration to the Sunbelt, the decline of the family farm, the entry of women into the labor force in large numbers, the rise of the women's movement, increasing divorce rates, and the changing family structure. Students should consider the connections between the modern women's movement and the women's rights movement of earlier decades. Which issues created the women's movement of the 1970s? Why did the Equal Rights Amendment fail? Selections from the writings of leading feminists and their opponents can be read and discussed. Attention should be paid to the major gains by women in education and in the workplace.

Major attention should be given to demographic changes and major social problems of contemporary America.

Finally, consideration should be given to the major social problems of contemporary America, including juvenile and adult crime, illegal use of drugs and alcohol, teenage pregnancy, and child neglect. Issues inherent in these problems can be debated, and experts from the community can be invited as speakers.

The United States in Recent Times

In this concluding unit students can place the recent past in historical perspective. At the end of this year's study, students should be able to discuss long-term trends and to assess their meaning. They should be aware of the influence of the Constitution on daily events in their community and nation and its continuing importance in defining the rights and freedoms of Americans.

The teacher should review the major events of the past decade, including the presidencies of Jimmy Carter and Ronald Reagan, and set

Students should be aware of the influence of the Constitution on daily events in their community and nation and its continuing importance in defining the rights and freedoms of Americans.

them in historical perspective. To what extent is foreign policy bipartisan? How might a president from another party handle a particular crisis; for example, the Middle East or the Iranian hostage crisis? What should be done about the national debt and deficit spending?

Much of the national political debate of the past two decades has been concerned with the expansion of the power of the federal government and the federal courts. This unit is intended to help students understand the extent to which such issues are rooted in the Progressive Era, the New Deal, and the civil rights movement. This is an appropriate time to reflect on the redefinition of the Bill of Rights during the twentieth century, particularly the tension between the rights of the individual and the power of the state. By examining such issues as drug testing, obscenity, abortion, and testing for AIDS, students should consider how the Constitution works today and compare contemporary practices to the vision of the Founding Fathers.

Contemporary economic and social conditions in the United States can be viewed with historical perspective. Students might compare the status of minorities in 1900 to that of the present and reflect on changes in job opportunities, educational opportunities, and legal protections available to minorities and women. How does the life of a new immigrant to the United States today compare with what it was in 1900? What is the condition of women's rights today compared to 1900? By viewing three generations of social and economic change, students can begin to assess the collective effects of the political and legal reforms that have been enacted since the Progressive Era.

Students should recognize that under our democratic political system the United States has achieved a level of freedom, political stability, and economic prosperity that has made it a model for other nations, the leader of the world's democratic societies, and a magnet for people all over the world who yearn for a life of freedom and opportunity. Students should understand that our rights and freedoms are not accidents of history. They are the result of a carefully defined set of political principles that are embodied in the Constitution. Students should recognize that our ability to debate our current and historical problems and to freely criticize our government is not a sign of weakness but is one of the hallmarks of a free society.

Students should see that the history of the United States has had special significance for the rest of the world, both because of its free political system and its pluralistic nature. In a world riven by ethnic, racial, and religious hatred, the United States has demonstrated the strength and dynamism of a racially, religiously, and culturally diverse people, united under a democratic political system.

Students should perceive these historic achievements in a global context. They should recognize the cynicism with which undemocratic regimes use the rhetoric of democracy while violating its most basic principles. They should understand that most nations today do not rest on the consent of the governed and do not guarantee their citizens basic rights and freedoms.

Students recognize that under our democratic political system the United States has achieved a level of freedom, political stability, and economic prosperity that has made it a leader of the world's democratic societies.

By the end of grade eleven, students should see the relevance of history to their daily lives and understand how the ideas and events of the past shape the institutions and debates of contemporary America. Living in a free society is a precious inheritance; it should not be taken for granted. Students should recognize that our democratic political system depends on them—as educated citizens—to survive and prosper.

■ Grade Twelve—
Principles of American Democracy (One Semester)

In this course students apply knowledge gained in previous years of study to pursue a deeper understanding of the institutions of American government. In addition, they draw on their studies of American history and of other societies to compare different systems of government in the world today. This course should be viewed as the culmination of the civic literacy strand that prepares students to vote, to reflect on the responsibilities of citizenship, and to participate in community activities.

This course is the culmination of the civic literacy strand that prepares students to vote, to reflect on the responsibilities of citizenship, and to participate in community activities.

The Constitution and the Bill of Rights

In this first study of the course, students focus on the philosophy of those who framed the Constitution and the Bill of Rights. Both documents are used in conjunction with selected portions of the *Federalist Papers*. Teachers should use the latter to illustrate such major constitutional concepts as separation of powers, checks and balances, and enumerated powers as well as the framers' understanding of human nature and the political process. For example, when dealing with the rationale for checks and balances and separation of powers, students should study *Federalist Paper Number 51;* or when dealing with the role of the judiciary, they should study *Federalist Paper Number 78*. Others should be used where appropriate.

Students focus on the philosophy of those who framed the Constitution and the Bill of Rights.

The *Federalist Papers* should be presented as arguments intended to persuade a skeptical public, rather than as holy writ, so that students can understand that the ideas now taken for granted had to survive close scrutiny.

The Federalist Papers *persuaded a skeptical public.*

The Courts and the Governmental Process

In this unit students examine the role of the courts as a major element in the governmental process. They should concentrate on how the courts have interpreted the Bill of Rights over time, with emphasis on themes such as due process of law and equal protection as guaranteed by the Fourteenth Amendment. Whenever possible, students should be given illustrations of the kinds of controversies that have arisen because of challenges or differing interpretations of the Bill of Rights. The unit should be organized around case studies of specific issues, such as the First Amendment's cases on free speech, religious liberty, separation of church and state, academic freedom, and the right of assembly. Supreme Court decisions may be debated or simulated in the classroom, following readings of orginal source materials, including significant excerpts from the specific cases. Students should understand not only that rights and societal interests were in conflict, but also that each case involved real people and that our present laws have resulted from the debates, trials, and sacrifices of ordinary people.

In examining the evolution of the civil rights issue under the equal protection clause, students should draw on their knowledge of the Civil War and the passage of the Reconstruction amendments. Students should examine the changing interpretation of civil rights law from the *Plessy* v. *Ferguson* decision of 1896 to the *Brown* decision of 1954. Although it is not possible to analyze every decision that marked the shift of the Supreme Court from 1896 to 1954, critical reading of the *Yick Wo* decision should serve to remind students that racial discrimination affected not only blacks but other groups as well, including Asians and Hispanics. A study of the higher education cases (for example, *Sweatt* v. *Painter* or *McLaurin* v. *Oklahoma*) should prepare the ground for the Court's switch in *Brown*. The *Brown* decision provides the opportunity to debate whether the law should be color blind or color conscious. Students can use materials from these cases to simulate a trial of the issues.

Our Government Today: The Legislative and Executive Branches

In this unit students examine the work of modern legislatures and the executive branch of government.

Each generation of Americans has made contributions to our governmental system, and citizens in each era have created mechanisms to deal with new problems and address inequities.

Case studies of recent issues (for example, tax reform, social security reform, and environmental protection laws) should be used to explore the process and issues of lawmaking, such as the committee system, lobbying, and the influence of the media and special interests on legislation. Through critical reading of primary documents and the use of simulations, role play, and other interactive learning strategies, students can practice critical thinking and apply these skills to assess proposed legislation, candidates for office, and the practices of legislatures.

Students should examine the workings of the executive branch. Through a critical reading of primary and secondary sources, students should be able to document the evolution of the Presidency and the growth of the power to cope with war, economic crisis, and America's role in world affairs. Through selected case studies, students can analyze presidential campaigns, the handling of international crises, and the scope and limits of presidential power (both foreign and domestic). Examples might include the Steel Crisis, the Cuban Missile Crisis, or the

Each generation of Americans has made contributions to our governmental system, and citizens in each era have created mechanisms to deal with new problems and address inequities.

104

Iran Hostage Crisis. Students should explore the process of presidential decision making through role play, simulation, and interactive learning.

Federalism: State and Local Government

In this unit students analyze the principles of federalism. Students should learn how power is divided among federal, state, and local governments. What kinds of issues does each level of government handle? What happens when there is overlapping jurisdiction; for example, on matters such as transportation and housing? How do people get involved in state and local government? How do state and local regulatory agencies differ from those at the federal level? Students should become aware of the important areas (for example, criminal justice, family law, environmental protection, and education) that remain largely under state and county control. They should discuss the important functions that are retained by localities, such as police and fire protection, sanitation, local public schools, and other services.

By analyzing a significant school policy issue, students should learn how public education is governed and financed and how policies that affect schools are influenced and decided. Students should examine topics such as the role of the local school board, state legislation, California initiatives affecting the schools, and the budgetary priorities of elected state officials. Students should analyze the importance of their vote in influencing the quality and future of public education in California and consider ways of becoming actively involved in issues that affect education.

Time should be devoted to a study of the ways in which individuals can become participatory citizens through voting, jury service, volunteerism, and involvement in community organizations. Resource people from local agencies and organizations can be invited to visit classrooms and facilitate site visits to demonstrate the work they do and reinforce the vital role the individual plays in community life. In addition, students should be given opportunities to volunteer for community service in their schools and communities.

Comparative Governments, with Emphasis on Communism in the World Today

This unit begins with a review of the major philosophies encountered by students during their previous studies: socialism, fascism, communism, capitalism, and democratic pluralism. Students should understand the way in which these different philosophies influence governments, economic policies, social welfare policies, and human rights practices. They should recognize that most nations combine aspects of different philosophies.

The fundamental differences between democracies and dictatorships of the right and the left should be understood. Critical thinking skills should be used to analyze the nature of a dictatorial regime in which no social contract exists between the state and those it governs and in which citizens have no rights nor means of redressing wrongs.

Under federalism, power is divided among federal, state, and local governments.

Time should be devoted to a study of the ways in which individuals can become participatory citizens through voting, jury service, volunteerism, and involvement in community organizations.

Students review the major philosophies: socialism, fascism, communism, capitalism, and democratic pluralism.

105

Does such a government rest on the consent of the governed? Do citizens have rights that the state must respect?

A review of pre-World War II fascism in Germany, Italy, Spain, and Portugal should be updated with a survey of contemporary dictatorships of the right; for example, the regimes in Paraguay and Chile; and the undemocratic reigns of leaders such as Ferdinand Marcos in the Philippines, Francois Duvalier in Haiti, and Idi Amin in Uganda. Attention should be given to the arbitrary rulings, torture, imprisonment, and executions without trials that attend fascist takeovers and help to maintain their control. Students should examine the social, economic, and political conditions that have given rise to such regimes. They should analyze the support given to such regimes by people who would protect or restore the status quo at any cost and by people who seek a military end to internal and imported revolutionary terrorism that their civilian governments have been unable to control. Attention also should be given to the democratic movement in such countries as Spain, Argentina, the Philippines, and South Korea.

Understanding the global nature of communism is essential.

The main focus of this unit is on communism because of its importance in the world today. Understanding the global nature of communism should be enhanced by map study and identification of communist governments in Asia, Africa, Latin America, and Eastern Europe. In discussing communism students should use what they learned in grade ten, with specific reference to the Russian Revolution, Marxist ideology, the dictatorship of Joseph Stalin, and the expansion of Soviet power after World War II. The nature of communist rule in the Soviet Union should be compared to communism in Cuba, Cambodia, Vietnam, Ethiopia, and China with attention to similarities and differences.

Students should examine the means by which communist regimes have come to power and the appeal that these regimes have for groups of the left who believe that only revolution or radical change can reform their societies. Students should understand the appeal of communist ideology to intellectuals and the poor.

Students should understand the concept of the total state where the government, the military, the educational system, all social organizations, the media, and the economy are controlled by the communist party. They should analyze the methods used by communist regimes to maintain control; for example, the repression of political opposition and dissident minorities through the use of internal controls such as the KGB and forced labor camps in the Gulag Archipelago where critics and dissident intellectuals are treated as criminals.

Students should examine the condition of human rights in communist societies: Why have communist revolutions been followed by purges of dissidents, mass arrests of political opponents, murder of "class enemies," suppression of free speech, abolition of private property, and attacks on religious groups? Why do many artists and intellectuals defect to noncommunist nations? Why do communist governments spy on their citizens and prevent them from emigrating? Why do they jail or harass critics of their government? Why is only one party allowed in a communist state? What significance does a one-party election have in a communist state? Why are independent trade unions not tolerated in a communist state? Why do ordinary people such as the Vietnamese boat people, Cuban refugees, and East Germans who scale the Berlin Wall risk their lives to flee a communist state? To assess the Soviet Union's pattern of dominating other nations, students should review the overthrow of the Czech government, the mass deportations and Russification of the Baltic populations, the Hungarian Revolution, the Berlin Wall, the suppression of the Solidarity movement in Poland, and the invasion of Afghanistan.

Students examine the condition of human rights in communist societies.

The economic record of communism should be assessed: What have been the effects of centralized planning? Students should analyze the effects of an economic system in which greater effort does not result in greater reward for the individual; in which individuals are not allowed to accumulate capital for future productivity; in which prices are not allowed to rise in order to reduce quantities demanded; and in which consumers have no control over allocation policies affecting the trade-off between consumer goods on one hand and military, defense, and police activities on the other. Recent changes in China and the Soviet Union that permit farmers to sell their crops for profit and that encourage small-scale entrepreneurial activities should be analyzed.

Contemporary Issues in the World Today

This course should conclude with an activity in which students analyze a major social issue. This activity might be a research paper in which students analyze a problem, marshal historical and social science evidence, provide a critique of alternative positions, and present their own position on the issue. A student could prepare this research as if it were a background paper for candidates in local, state, or national elections or as if the student were developing reasons for choosing among candidates.

Among the topics that might be addressed are technological issues, such as nuclear arms proliferation and arms control; environmental issues, such as acid rain, toxic waste disposal, and resource depletion; human rights issues; economic issues, such as competition from abroad, either because of cheap labor or advanced technology; health issues, such as drug abuse and the spread of AIDS; international economic issues, such as the movement to decentralize socialist economies; and international political issues stemming from the demand for democratic government in nations of Latin America and Southeast Asia. Students should pay attention to the global context of these issues as well as their importance in local, state, or national affairs.

The course concludes with an activity in which students analyze a major social issue; e.g., research papers with their own positions on the issue presented at a schoolwide consortium.

At the conclusion of this unit, a schoolwide consortium might be planned in which students present their papers in open forum and debate or discuss the issues from alternative viewpoints.

107

■ Grade Twelve—
Economics (One Semester)

In a one-semester course in economics, students should deepen their understanding of the economic problems and institutions of the nation and world in which they live. They should learn to make reasoned decisions on economic issues as citizens, workers, consumers, business owners and managers, and members of civic groups. In this capstone course students should add to the economic understandings they acquired in previous grades and apply tools (such as graphs, statistics, and equations) learned in other subject fields to their understanding of our economic system.

This course primarily is a course in social science, enriching students' understanding of the operations and institutions of economic systems, rather than a course in household or business management or budgeting. Throughout this course, measurement concepts and methods should be introduced; for example, tables, charts, graphs, ratios, percentages, and index numbers. Behind every graph is an equation or set of equations that specifies a relationship among economic variables. Thus, to master the economic method, students must use graphs and understand, at the appropriate level, the mathematical equations they represent.

Fundamental Economic Concepts

The basic economic problem facing all individuals, groups, and nations is the problem of scarcity. Scarcity results from the limited natural resources, such as water, land, and minerals, that are available to produce the variety of goods and services that we need and want. Because of scarcity, choices must be made concerning how to utilize limited resources. In this unit students should learn the difference between the final goods and services that any economy produces and the productive resources, including human resources, capital goods, and natural resources, that are used to produce these final goods and services. They should learn and then apply a reasoned approach to making decisions.

The basic choices that producers in any economic system must make involve determining what goods and services to produce, how to produce these goods and services, and for whom to produce them. Students should be introduced to our largely free market system that uses prices and levels of supply and demand in markets to answer these basic questions. Households, including individuals, demand the goods and services that give them the most satisfaction, given their income and the prices of these goods. Business firms try to maximize profits by supplying at the least cost the goods and services that households demand.

Students deepen their understanding of the economic problems and institutions of the nation and world in which they live and learn to make reasoned decisions on economic issues.

Basic economic problems facing all individuals, groups, and nations include scarcity, choices, and economic efficiency.

Businesses allocate factors of production based on the demand for the goods and services they produce. This "derived demand" for factors is a major determinant of distribution of income in a market economy.

Economic efficiency requires that individuals and business firms specialize in the performance of particular tasks or the manufacture of particular goods and that they exchange their surpluses of goods for the goods they want to consume. Money was developed to facilitate this exchange. Thus, specialization, exchange, and money are the results of our interdependence, which, in turn, results in efficient production of the final goods and services of our economy.

Comparative Economic Systems

A market system is characterized by decentralized decision making on the part of households and businesses. In this free enterprise system, most of the goods and services are produced by the private sector, by firms owned and operated for profit. The decisions of individuals influence market prices that reflect the preferences of all participants and that act as signals to producers and as rationing devices. Thus, to answer the basic economic questions, decision makers in the market system rely primarily on the preferences and choices of the members of the society.

Students should learn about alternatives to the market system, such as traditional and command economies, and learn how decisions in these economies rely on mechanisms other than the choices of the members of these societies. Students should learn that no real world economy is a pure form of any of these economies. They should understand that decentralized decision making in a market is most evident in the economy of the United States, Canada, and Western Europe, whereas elements of command economy are most evident in the Soviet Union. They should learn that economic systems change to reflect changes in values or technology and in the role of the market and the government. Students should study the strengths and weaknesses of each society and its values regarding the objectives of an economic system.

Students learn about alternatives to the market system, such as traditional and command economies, and learn how decisions in these economies rely on mechanisms other than the choices of the members of these societies.

Microeconomics

In this unit students should examine the operations of markets. They should learn how prices and the quantity demanded and supplied are determined in the markets for goods and factors of production. They should study how prices provide information and incentives and serve to ration limited resources. Students should learn about the interaction of the demand schedule and the curve which represents it together with the supply schedule and its graphic representation in determining prices and output. They also should learn what events lead to changes in demand and supply and how these changes influence prices.

Students should learn about alternative forms of business organizations, including single proprietorships, partnerships, and corporations, and their impact on the economy. They should consider in detail the operations of the labor market. Students should analyze the determinants of the level of employment and wages in different occupations and the impact of unionization, the minimum wage, and unemployment insurance.

Microeconomics is the study of individual behavior in the economy.

Students should focus specifically on the distribution of income in our economy, the differing costs of living across the United States, and the determination of income and cost distribution. Students should be aware of alternative measures of this distribution and the methods that federal, state, and local governments use to influence income distribution through transfer payments and taxes.

Our market economy is characterized by different market structures, including monopolies and oligopolies, and various economic principles, such as monopolistic competition and perfect competition. Students should learn how less than perfectly competitive markets operate and examine their impact on the economy. They should also learn that a pure market economy has disadvantages, including its failure to provide goods and services that are consumed jointly or that benefit people who do not have to pay for them directly. These goods and services include clean air, education, national defense, and roads. Students should consider the role of the government in a largely free market economy. Students should examine other responsibilities of the government, including establishing trade regulations and price controls and influencing the market's equilibrium. The role of the government in agriculture can be introduced as a case study of government intervention in a market.

Macroeconomics

Macroeconomics is the functioning of our economy as a whole. To facilitate their understanding of macroeconomics and deepen their understanding of the nature and history of our economy, students should learn about the statistics that have been developed to measure the functioning of our economy, including measures of national income (such as the gross national product) and measures of change in the price level (such as the consumer price index and the gross national product deflator). Students should use these statistics and measures of employment and unemployment to study the business cycle, unemployment, inflation, and economic growth.

Aggregate demand in our economy is determined by decisions of households on consumption, of businesses on investment, of purchasers of our goods abroad, and of the government. Students should learn about the factors that determine each of these components of aggregate demand. Teachers should emphasize that fiscal policy involves government spending and taxing actions to stabilize the economy. Students should understand how this policy is determined and how it operates. They should understand the federal budget process. They should be able to discuss the meaning of the government budget deficit and the government debt and how these factors influence the economy.

Monetary policy influences aggregate demand. The course covers the creation of money, the role of the Federal Reserve in the creation of money and monetary policy, and the role of financial intermediaries in our economy. Students should understand the purposes and economic effects of these financial institutions.

Aggregate supply is the total amount of goods and services produced in the economy during a given period of time. The upper limit on aggregate supply is the productive capacity of our economy. Increasing this capacity requires giving up consumption today for future benefits; for example, a student postponing working to acquire more education, a business retaining earnings to reinvest rather than distributing these earnings as dividends, and government acting to raise taxes.

International Economic Concepts

In this final unit students should concentrate on the differences between intranational and international trade. They should learn about foreign exchange and how exchange rates are determined. Students should learn why nations trade internationally, and they should understand comparative and absolute advantage. They should apply what they learned about specialization and exchange in the first unit of the course to the field of international trade.

Students concentrate on the characteristics of and the differences between intranational and international trade.

The balance of payments and the balance of trade are measures of the performance of countries in the international market. Students should learn about the meaning of these measures and what is included in them. Governments influence the pattern of imports and exports by tariffs, quotas, and other trade restrictions. Students should learn the reasons for these policies and how such policies affect the sectors of the economy that are being protected and the nation as a whole.

Finally, students might review their tenth-grade studies of developing nations and consider what factors, conditions, and policies help them to achieve sustained economic growth. They should apply to other nations what they have learned about supply and growth in our economy.

Students might review their tenth-grade studies of developing nations and consider what factors, conditions, and policies help these nations to achieve sustained economic growth.

Criteria for Evaluating Instructional Materials

Criteria for Evaluating Instructional Materials

*T*HE potential of this framework to influence classroom activities depends to a large extent on the quality of the textbooks and other instructional materials selected. Textbooks that are written in a laborious or disconnected style will undermine the history–social science curriculum, but thoughtful, interesting accounts will support teachers' efforts to bring the goals of the history–social science program to life. The following evaluation standards are intended to assist publishers in developing the kind of instructional materials that implement the purposes of this framework. These criteria should serve as standards for the statewide adoption of instructional materials in kindergarten and grades one through eight; they also can be used as guidelines in preparing and reviewing instructional materials for grades nine through twelve. In addition to the following criteria, publishers should note with care the relevant portions of the California *Education Code* and the requirements of the 1986 edition of the *Standards for Evaluation of Instructional Materials with Respect to Social Content*.

Basic Guidelines

The basic guidelines to be used in considering textbooks and other instructional materials are as follows:

1. Textbooks and other instructional materials must reflect the clearly stated characteristics, goals, strands, and course descriptions of this framework. Print and nonprint materials must present history and geography in a holistic manner, integrated with the humanities and the social sciences. Time and

place are central to each setting. The life of a people must be depicted with empathy (as they saw themselves, through literature and other contemporary accounts); with perspective (as provided by the social sciences); and with persistent attention to the ethical beliefs and values that illuminate the life of a civilization and that speak in universal terms to our own time.

2. Instructional materials should present history as an exciting and fascinating story as do books and films that are prepared for a general audience. The difference between students and a general audience is that a general audience is not compelled to read boring material; students often are. Materials that students can read (or view or use) with interest, enthusiasm, and pleasure are needed. The materials for the classroom should compare favorably with the books, magazines, software, and educational television programs that are available to students outside school.

3. The writing (or other form of presentation) should be vivid and dramatic without sacrificing accuracy; it should incorporate human interest wherever possible so that students will recognize the universal humanity of people in other times and places. The story should focus on the men and women whose triumphs and tragedies continue to deserve our attention; it should convey a lively sense of people who struggled, failed, achieved great things, authored terrible tragedies, labored in anonymity, or strode boldly on the stage of history. Whatever the story to be told—the forming of a new nation, the collapse of an ancient civilization, the clash of nations in world war—the story should have continuity, narrative coherence, an element of suspense, and other qualities of well-written history based on the best and most recent scholarship.

4. Superficial skimming of key facts and the mere mention of major topics and significant individuals are not acceptable. Once chosen for discussion, a topic must be presented in depth, with a beginning, a middle, and an end; and it must be presented with careful attention to the skillful interweaving of history, geography, the humanities, and the perspective of the social sciences. Publishers at all times must think of their readers (or viewers) as an audience, whose interest, attention, and respect must be earned and held.

5. Materials must be accurate and truthful in describing controversies in history, including controversies among historians. The past, like the present, was rife with controversy, with hotly contested events, with uncertainty and division among major actors, with indecision on the part of policymakers, and with attacks on the reputation of now-revered figures. The past cannot be brought to life if it is presented as a desiccated version of reality stripped of the debates, confusion, and discord that divided contemporaries.

6. Whether treating past or present, textbooks and other instructional materials must portray the experiences of men, women, children, and youth as well as of different racial, religious, and ethnic groups. Both in United States history and in world history, the interaction of groups deserves careful attention. Whether they conflict with one another, cooperate, or live in relative isolation, diverse cultural groups must be depicted accurately as actors on the historical stage. Materials that ignore the importance of cultural diversity in United States history or world history are unacceptable.

7. Historical controversies must display a variety of perspectives by the participants. Colonialism in the nineteenth century, for example, should be seen both through the eyes of the rulers and the eyes of the ruled, and the accounts of wars should convey the perspectives of both the conquerors and the conquered. Differences of opinion should be fully aired, for example, when considering the debate over slavery at the Constitutional Convention, implementation of the *Brown* decision, and issues of the nuclear age.

8. Writers of history textbooks and other instructional materials must pay close attention to ethical issues. The writers should delineate the ethical ideas developed by different people in history, either as religious or secular belief systems, and they should consider the ethical principles at stake in historical events and controversies. Through their study of history, students should have many opportunities to consider standards of ethical behavior. And publishers and other developers of curriculum materials should pay special attention to the treatment of human rights as an expression of a society's ethics.

9. Instructional materials should include primary source materials to enable students to get an authentic sense of other times and places. These materials might be in the form of excerpts from autobiographies, speeches, court decisions, diaries, essays, sacred literature, or other documentation. As much as possible, this material should be blended with the narrative of the textbook so that it serves as a voice from the past, bringing the narrative to life. Extracts from all periods of history should be chosen for their historical value and their intrinsic interest. Some examples are poems of children in concentration camps during the Holocaust, diaries of pioneers who crossed the Great Plains, and narratives of slaves.

10. Materials should reflect the significance of civic values and democratic institutions. When they deal with United States history, the writers of these materials should pay close attention to the evolution of basic democratic principles, such as universal suffrage, freedom of the press, freedom of religion, freedom of speech, the right to due process, universal education, respect for the rights of minorities, and other hallmarks of a democratic society. Those instructional materials that deal with

world history should describe the balance between the power of the state and the rights of the citizens and should note the presence or absence of those practices that are associated with a democratic government.

11. Materials should reflect the importance of education in a democratic society. Not only should these materials show the role and history of educational institutions in preparing citizens for life in a democratic society, but also they should present models of intellectual accomplishment. Students should see numerous examples of men and women who used their learning and intelligence to make important contributions to society. Students should understand that great advances in science and technology, as well as in democratic thought, were made possible by educated minds and that freedom and prosperity depend on the intellect and character of a nation's citizens. Students should discover through their instructional materials that in the lives of individuals and in the life of society, education is power.

12. Materials should incorporate the use of literature or should refer to literature in other sources. Whether in poetry, drama, prose, or fiction, people throughout history have used language to express their hopes, fears, and dreams. Instructional materials should draw on literature as a resource to demonstrate the inner life of people in other times and places.

13. Materials that deal with American life and history should include patriotic emphases, not of a jingoistic, chauvinistic sort but calculated to inspire understanding of and commitment to the best principles in the American heritage. For example, there should be examples of memorable addresses by historic figures, such as George Washington, Patrick Henry, Abraham Lincoln, Frederick Douglass, Susan B. Anthony, Franklin D. Roosevelt, Martin Luther King, Jr., and John F. Kennedy. There should be excerpts from the Constitution and the Bill of Rights; major decisions of the United States Supreme Court; and notable poems, songs, and legends that have helped to create a vision of the United States as a nation that is committed to equality, justice, and freedom for all its citizens.

14. Textbook publishers in particular should be encouraged to adopt formats other than a single, heavy hardbound book. Books of several hundred pages can be daunting to students; their very weightiness may defeat the effort to create engaging, lively materials. Alternative formats, such as small hardbound or softcover books or pamphlets, each of which presents a rich and complete story, diary excerpts, biographies, and so forth, will be viewed with favor. The written instructional materials for all the courses in this framework might be prepared as sets of books, with individual books for each unit within each course. This would allow teachers greater flexibility in determining the emphasis and timing of their course content; it

would facilitate future revisions by publishers; and it would permit the assembly of books that might be tailored to the local requirements of school districts in other states.

15. Teachers' materials intended for use with instructional materials should include examples of creative assignments, suggestions for significant questions and emphases based on the content of the lesson, a bibliography of supplementary readings and films, and alternative strategies for teaching concepts and skills. These materials should avoid condescension or pseudo-technical approaches to the content. Teachers are well-educated, skilled professionals who need a lively and supportive text.

The ultimate test of any textbook or instructional material is its power to engage the imagination of the reader. No matter how graphically the textbooks are illustrated, no matter how many experts are hired to certify their validity, and no matter how many claims are made on their behalf as conveyers of skills and concepts, the textbooks will fail unless they excite the enthusiasm of the students who read them.

Organization of Materials

The instructional materials should provide:

1. An organizational structure for textbooks that includes a preface or introduction, table of contents, index, glossary, appropriate activities to reinforce students' learning, and primary sources that illustrate the content

2. A preface or introduction to the student's edition of the textbook and a description of the organizational structure of the text, including its special features, point of view, goals and objectives, conceptual design, and distinguishing features that can serve as a helpful orientation for students, teachers, and parents

3. Extended activities for home study

4. Alignment of all elements of the instructional materials, such as the student's textbook, teacher's manual, and software, into an integrated, constructive, and purposeful basal program with thematic coherence

5. A format for printed materials that incorporates research relative to features that best promote reading comprehension, learning, and retention

6. Activities for each area to be studied that are appropriate for use by students with a wide range of abilities

7. End-of-chapter materials that focus on significant concepts within the chapter and relate these to the maturity and interests of the students for whom the material has been written

8. A variety of maps (including topographic maps) that are up-to-date and accurate and that provide clearly understandable legends illustrating the five major geographic themes

9. Coordination of all graphics, images, pictures, and source materials with the theme or topic under study

10. A glossary within the student's textbook that contains significant vocabulary words and terms that are highlighted in the narrative
11. Opportunities through interactive experiences, using technology where practical, for students to practice decision-making and action-taking skills and to reflect on the resulting consequences
12. A variety of ways to extend the learning process beyond the textbooks (Technology and telecommunications provide excellent opportunities to bring specific content-related information to the learning environment.)

Teachers' Manuals and Reference Materials

The teachers' manuals and reference materials for the program must include:

1. A teaching guide of convenient size and format for use with an overview and/or summary for each unit
2. Goals, objectives, and a variety of evaluation components for each unit, all closely correlated with the student's text
3. Instructional opportunities for teaching students of different cultural backgrounds
4. Suggestions for individual and group activities, such as cooperative learning in which students help each other
5. Examples of creative assignments
6. Background materials for the use of technology-related tools, with recommendations for incorporating a wide variety of technology with options for assessing the quality of materials
7. A variety of ways to extend students' learning beyond the textbook, including a bibliography of professional references, resources, and supplemental activities
8. Instructional approaches for meeting the needs of less-prepared, gifted, limited-English-proficient, or special education students and those with different learning styles
9. Suggestions for extending the program by involving parents and members of the community

Assessment and Evaluation

The assessment and evaluation features of the program must include:

1. Opportunities for assessment of students' progress not only in knowledge but also in basic skills and abilities, including thinking and social participation
2. A variety of evaluative techniques, including the teacher's evaluation of the students' performance, students' evaluation of personal progress, and peer evaluation
3. Opportunities for students to make oral and written reports in which they are encouraged to state a position and support it
4. Assessment and evaluation components for each area evaluated by the California Assessment Program: United States his-

tory, citizenship, government, world history, geography, economics, basic study skills, and critical thinking skills

Instructional Media

The instructional media for the program must include:

1. Visual nonprint materials such as films, videotapes, filmstrips, charts, maps, archival items, or reproductions that are:
   a. Accurate, objective, current, and appropriate
   b. Responsive to the needs and comprehension of pupils at their respective grade levels
   c. Developed with good teaching principles and with a high interest level for students
2. Materials designed for auditory use, such as records and tapes, must meet the following criteria:
   a. Be appropriate in content and length for student learners.
   b. Use voices that are clear and appropriate for the role portrayed.
   c. Use standard English with speakers selected for appropriateness of role presentation.
3. Technology-related materials such as instructional television, computer software, and interactive videodisc programs must be integrally related to other instructional materials as a basal (text) replacement or as a necessary part of an instructional materials system. In addition, electronic media must:
   a. Meet the standards for exemplary software as presented in *Guidelines for Educational Software in California Schools.*[1]
   b. In the case of technological tools, such as databases, database managers, spreadsheets, and electronic communication packages, be available in multiple machine or operating system formats.
   c. Exemplify uses of technology that are primary methodological tools in the social sciences.
   d. Exemplify the influence that information technologies have had on the study and understanding of geography, economics, and the other social sciences.

[1] *Guidelines for Educational Software in California Schools.* Sacramento: California State Department of Education, 1985. Copies may be obtained from the Educational Technology Unit, California State Department of Education; telephone (916) 445-5065.

Publications Available from the Department of Education

This publication is one of over 600 that are available from the California Department of Education. Some of the more recent publications or those most widely used are the following:

Item No.	Title (Date of publication)	Price
1063	Adoption Recommendations of the Curriculum Development and Supplemental Materials Commission, 1992: California Basic Instructional Materials in Science (1992)	$5.50
0883	The Ages of Infancy: Caring for Young, Mobile, and Older Infants (videocassette and guide) (1990)*	65.00
0973	The American Indian: Yesterday, Today, and Tomorrow (1991)	6.50
1012	Attendance Accounting and Reporting in California Public Schools (1991)	5.50
1079	Beyond Retention: A Study of Retention Rates, Practices, and Successful Alternatives in California (1993)	4.25
0972	California Assessment Program: A Sampler of Mathematics Assessment (1991)	5.00
0912	California State Plan for Carl D. Perkins Vocational and Applied Technology Education Act Funds, 1991–1994 (1991)	13.00
1067	California Private School Directory, 1993-94 (1993)	16.00
1074	California Public School Directory (1993)	16.00
1017	California State Plan for the Child Care and Development Services Funded Under Federal Block Grant (1991)	5.50
1036	California Strategic Plan for Parental Involvement in Education (1992)	5.75
0488	Caught in the Middle: Educational Reform for Young Adolescents in California Public Schools (1987)	6.75
0874	The Changing History–Social Science Curriculum: A Booklet for Parents (1990)	10/5.00†
1053	The Changing History–Social Science Curriculum: A Booklet for Parents (Spanish) (1993)	10/5.00†
0867	The Changing Language Arts Curriculum: A Booklet for Parents (1990)	10/5.00†
1115	The Changing Language Arts Curriculum: A Booklet for Parents (Korean) (1993)	10/5.00†
0928	The Changing Language Arts Curriculum: A Booklet for Parents (Spanish Edition) (1991)	10/5.00†
0777	The Changing Mathematics Curriculum: A Booklet for Parents (1989)	10/5.00†
0891	The Changing Mathematics Curriculum: A Booklet for Parents (Spanish Edition) (1991)	10/5.00†
1072	Commodity Administrative Manual (1993)	13.00
0978	Course Models for the History–Social Science Framework, Grade Five—United States History and Geography: Making a New Nation (1991)	8.50
1034	Course Models for the History–Social Science Framework, Grade Six—World History and Geography: Ancient Civilizations (1993)	9.50
1045	Discoveries of Infancy: Cognitive Development and Learning (videocassette and guide) (1992)*	65.00
0976	Economic Education Mandate: Handbook for Survival (1991)	7.75
1046	English-as-a-Second-Language Model Standards for Adult Education Programs (1992)	7.00
0041	English–Language Arts Framework for California Public Schools (1987)	5.00
0927	English–Language Arts Model Curriculum Standards: Grades Nine Through Twelve (1991)	6.00
0987	ESEA, Chapter 2, Manual of Information (1991)	5.00
1056	Essential Connections: Ten Keys to Culturally Sensitive Care (videocassette and guide) (1993)*	65.00
1011	Exemplary Program Standards for Child Care Development Programs Serving Preschool and School-Age Children (1991)	5.50
0751	First Moves: Welcoming a Child to a New Caregiving Setting (videocassette and guide) (1988)*	65.00
0839	Flexible, Fearful, or Feisty: The Different Temperaments of Infants and Toddlers (videocassette and guide) (1990)*	65.00
0804	Foreign Language Framework for California Public Schools (1989)	6.50
0809	Getting in Tune: Creating Nurturing Relationships with Infants and Toddlers (videocassette and guide) (1990)*	65.00
1080	Guide and Criteria for Program Quality Review—Elementary (1993)	9.00
1078	Guide and Criteria for Program Quality Review—Middle Level (1993)	10.00
0986	Handbook for Teaching Korean-American Students (1991)‡	5.50
0734	Here They Come: Ready or Not—Report of the School Readiness Task Force (Full Report) (1988)	5.50
0712	History–Social Science Framework for California Public Schools (1988)	7.75
0750	Infant/Toddler Caregiving: An Annotated Guide to Media Training Materials (1989)	9.50
0878	Infant/Toddler Caregiving: A Guide to Creating Partnerships with Parents (1990)	10.00
0880	Infant/Toddler Caregiving: A Guide to Language Development and Communication (1990)	10.00
0877	Infant/Toddler Caregiving: A Guide to Routines (1990)	10.00
0879	Infant/Toddler Caregiving: A Guide to Setting Up Environments (1990)	10.00
0876	Infant/Toddler Caregiving: A Guide to Social–Emotional Growth and Socialization (1990)	10.00
1070	Instructional Materials Approved for Legal Compliance (1993)	10.50
1024	It's Elementary! Elementary Grades Task Force Report (1992)	6.50
0869	It's Not Just Routine: Feeding, Diapering, and Napping Infants and Toddlers (videocassette and guide) (1990)*	65.00
1107	Literature for History–Social Science, Kindergarten Through Grade Eight (1993)	8.00
1066	Literature for Science and Mathematics (1993)	9.50

*Videocassette also available in Chinese (Cantonese) and Spanish at the same price.

†The price for 100 booklets is $30; the price for 1,000 booklets is $230. A set of one of each of the parent booklets in English is $3; a set in Spanish is also $3.

‡Also available at the same price for students who speak Cantonese, Japanese, Pilipino, and Portuguese.

Item No.	Title (Date of publication)	Price
1033	Mathematics Framework for California Public Schools, 1992 Edition (1992)	$6.75
0929	Model Curriculum Standards, Grades Nine Through Twelve (1985)	5.50
0968	Moral and Civic Education and Teaching About Religion (1991 Revised Edition)	4.25
0969	Not Schools Alone: Guidelines for Schools and Communities to Prevent the Use of Tobacco, Alcohol, and Other Drugs Among Children and Youth (1991)	4.25
0974	Parent Involvement Programs in California Public Schools (1991)	6.75
0845	Physical Education Model Curriculum Standards, Grades Nine Through Twelve (1991)	5.50
1032	Program Guidelines for Individuals Who Are Severely Orthopedically Impaired (1992)	8.00
0906	Quality Criteria for High Schools: Planning, Implementing, Self-Study, and Program Quality Review (1990)	5.00
0979	Readings for the Christopher Columbus Quincentenary (1992)	2.75*
1048	Read to Me: Recommended Readings for Children Ages Two Through Seven (1992)	5.50
0831	Recommended Literature, Grades Nine Through Twelve (1990)	5.50
0895	Recommended Readings in Spanish Literature: Kindergarten Through Grade Eight (1991)	4.25
0753	Respectfully Yours: Magda Gerber's Approach to Professional Infant/Toddler Care (videocassette and guide) (1988)†	65.00
1042	School Nutrition Facility Planning Guide (1992)	8.00
1038	Science Facilities Design in California Public Schools (1992)	6.25
0870	Science Framework for California Public Schools (1990)	8.00
1040	Second to None: A Vision of the New California High School (1992)	5.75
0926	Seeing Fractions: A Unit for the Upper Elementary Grades (1991)	7.50
0970	Self-assessment Guide for School District Fiscal Policy Teams: Facilities Planning and Construction (1991)	4.50
0980	Simplified Buying Guide: Child and Adult Care Food Program (1992)	8.50
0752	Space to Grow: Creating a Child Care Environment for Infants and Toddlers (videocassette and guide) (1988)†	65.00
1014	Strategic Plan for Information Technology (1991)	4.50
1043	Success for Beginning Teachers: The California New Teacher Project, 1988–1992 (1992)	5.50
0920	Suggested Copyright Policy and Guidelines for California's School Districts (1991)	3.00‡
1044	Together in Care: Meeting the Intimacy Needs of Infants and Toddlers in Groups (videocassette and guide) (1992)†	65.00
0846	Toward a State of Esteem: The Final Report of the California Task Force to Promote Self-esteem and Personal and Social Responsibility (1990)	5.00
0758	Visions for Infant/Toddler Care: Guidelines for Professional Caregiving (1989)	6.50
0805	Visual and Performing Arts Framework for California Public Schools (1989)	7.25
1016	With History–Social Science for All: Access for Every Student (1992)	5.50
0989	Work Permit Handbook (1991)	7.75
1073	Writing Assessment Handbook: High School (1993)	9.25

*Also available in quantities of 10 for $7.50 (item number 9875); 30 for $20 (9876); and 100 for $60 (9877).
†Videocassette also available in Chinese (Cantonese) and Spanish at the same price.
‡Also available in quantities of 10 for $12.50 (item number 9940); 50 for $55 (9941); and 100 for $100 (9942).

Orders should be directed to:

California Department of Education
Bureau of Publications, Sales Unit
P.O. Box 271
Sacramento, CA 95812-0271

Please include the item number for each title ordered.

Mail orders must be accompanied by a check, a purchase order, or a credit card number, including expiration date (VISA or MasterCard only). Purchase orders without checks are accepted from governmental agencies only. Telephone orders will be accepted toll-free (1-800-995-4099) for credit card purchases only. Sales tax should be added to all orders from California purchasers. Stated prices, which include shipping charges to anywhere in the United States, are subject to change.

A complete list of publications available from the Department, including apprenticeship instructional materials, may be obtained by writing to the address listed above or by calling (916) 445-1260.

WK3 P.2-26
WK4 P.27-61

R93-47 (Ninth printing) 000-0081-93 300 1-94 17,500
94 84835